ZEPHANIAH
Judgment and Hope

Richard Caldwell

**KRESS
BIBLICAL
RESOURCES**

ISBN: 978-1-934952-44-3

DEDICATION

To the Elders at Founders Baptist Church. Your faithful ministry and friendship is a joy to my heart and strength for service.

Contents

1 More than Reformation (1:1) 1

   The Man Zephaniah (1:1) 4

   The Ministry of Zephaniah (1:1) 4

   Two Things of Which We Can Be Certain 5

   The Message of Zephaniah (Briefly) 6

   Application 7

2 Judgment Now and Judgment to Come (1:2-13) 10

   The Announcement of God's Wrath 11

   Zephaniah's Message to Us 13

   The Explanation for God's Wrath 13

   The Sacrifice of God 15

   Applying It 17

3 Only God Can Save From God (1:14-2:3) 19

   The Description of God's Judgment (1:14-18) 20

   The Answer for God's Judgment (2:1-3) 24

4 Judgment on the Nations (2:4-15) 26

   Judgments Upon the Surrounding Nations (2:4-15) 27

   The Judgments and God's Ultimate Purpose (2:11) 30

   Timeless Lessons from These Judgment Pronouncements 31

5 On the Brink of Ruin (3:1-8) 32

God Announces Judgment on the City Known By His Name. 32

A Summary of Sins that Deserve God's Judgment (3:1) 34

Manifestations of the Sins that Deserve God's Judgment (3:2-5) 34

God's Dealings with Sinful Men Should Lead Us to Repentance (3:6-8)
.... 40

6 The Promise of Salvation (3:9-13) 46

God's Saving Work Will Produce United Worshippers (3:9) 48

God's Saving Work Will Produce Resurrection Life (3:10) 51

God's Saving Work Will Produce Humility (3:11-12a) 52

God's Saving Work Will Produce Peace (3:12-13) 53

7 The Song of Salvation (3:14-20) 54

The Day of Salvation Is a Day of Exuberant Joy (3:14) 55

The Day of Salvation Is a Day of Gracious Deliverance (3:15) 57

The Day of Salvation Is a Day of Glorious Comfort (3:16-20) 60

8 Study Guide 63

ABOUT THE AUTHOR 70

ACKNOWLEDGMENTS

I am thankful for Larry Lartigue. He is a tireless worker for Christ's church, and a loyal friend. His years of work on behalf of sermons has been a treasure.

1
MORE THAN REFORMATION
(1:1)

The little book of Zephaniah carries a big message that has profound application for today's church. Zephaniah tells us that the important kingdom is the Lord's kingdom, not ours (not our nation's, not our party's, not our church's). It also tells us what we need far more than reformation. We need transformation. And Zephaniah insists that the transformation must include repentance.

Zephaniah declares his message during the reign of King Josiah of Judah, who succeeds Kings Manasseh (697-642 BC) and Amon (642-640 BC). Under Manasseh and Amon, Judah had known 57 years of tremendous spiritual and political darkness. **Manasseh** did great evil in the sight of the Lord. Hezekiah, his father, was, in many ways, a good king. However, from the time that Manasseh was 12 years old and took the throne, until he died at 67 years of age, Manasseh was most famous for bringing more wickedness on the land than the original pagan inhabitants that the Lord had driven out.

2 Chronicles 33:9 *Manasseh led Judah and the inhabitants of Jerusalem astray, to do more evil than the nations whom the LORD destroyed before the people of Israel.*

He not only brought about unsurpassed idolatry in the land of Judah, including building altars to false gods in the temple complex itself, but his wickedness extended to the sacrifice of his own sons.

1

2 Chronicles 33:1 *Manasseh was twelve years old when he began to reign, and he reigned fifty-five years in Jerusalem. ² And he did what was evil in the sight of the LORD, according to the abominations of the nations whom the LORD drove out before the people of Israel. ³ For he rebuilt the high places that his father Hezekiah had broken down, and he erected altars to the Baals, and made Asheroth, and worshiped all the host of heaven and served them. And he built altars in the house of the LORD, of which the LORD had said, "In Jerusalem shall my name be forever." ⁵ And he built altars for all the host of heaven in the two courts of the house of the LORD. ⁶ And he burned his sons as an offering in the Valley of the Son of Hinnom, and used fortune-telling and omens and sorcery, and dealt with mediums and with necromancers. He did much evil in the sight of the LORD, provoking him to anger.*

2 Chronicles tells us that after the Assyrians captured him, Manasseh pleaded with the God of his fathers for mercy. God had compassion upon him, and he returned to Jerusalem.

2 Chronicles 33:10 *The LORD spoke to Manasseh and to his people, but they paid no attention. ¹¹ Therefore the LORD brought upon them the commanders of the army of the king of Assyria, who captured Manasseh with hooks and bound him with chains of bronze and brought him to Babylon. ¹² And when he was in distress, he entreated the favor of the LORD his God and humbled himself greatly before the God of his fathers. ¹³ He prayed to him, and God was moved by his entreaty and heard his plea and brought him again to Jerusalem into his kingdom. Then Manasseh knew that the LORD was God.*

But the damage was done, even though he commanded Judah to serve the Lord.

2 Chronicles 33:15 *And he took away the foreign gods and the idol from the house of the LORD, and all the altars that he had built on the mountain of the house of the LORD and in Jerusalem, and he threw them outside of the city. ¹⁶ He also restored the altar of the LORD and offered on it sacrifices of peace offerings and of thanksgiving, and he commanded Judah to serve the LORD, the God of Israel. ¹⁷ Nevertheless, the people still sacrificed at the high places, but only to the LORD their God.*

Manasseh was succeeded by his wicked son **Amon** (642 - 640 B.C.), who followed the worst in his father.

2 Chronicles 33:21 *Amon was twenty-two years old when he began to reign, and he reigned two years in Jerusalem. ²² And he did what was evil in the sight of the LORD, as Manasseh his father had done. Amon sacrificed to all the images that Manasseh his father had made, and served them. ²³ And he did not humble himself before the LORD,* *as Manasseh his father had humbled himself, but this **Amon incurred guilt more and more.** ²⁴ **And his servants conspired against him and put him to death in his house.*** ²⁵ But the people of the land struck down all those who had conspired against King Amon. **And the people of the land made Josiah his son king in his place.***

When **Josiah** came to the throne, he was 8 years old. Assyria, which previously conquered the northern kingdom of Israel, was already in massive decline. It was 640 B.C. when Josiah took the throne, and Assyria would lose its grip on Babylon by 626 and its grip on the Medes by 625. Nineveh, Assyria's capital city, was destroyed by a coalition of Medes and Babylonians in 612 B.C. By 605 B.C., about four years after Josiah's death, Assyria's empire was over.

This Assyrian weakness gave Josiah the opportunity not only to cast off the worship of false gods, specifically the worship characteristic of the Assyrians, but to begin to embrace the hope of reclaiming territories lost to the Assyrians in the north. There must have been some people early in Josiah's life who wanted the sort of reforms that came to characterize his reign, because when someone is 8 years old, the decisions are mostly made by others. When Josiah was 16 years old, the Lord did a great work in his heart. As a result, he led in a great reform that began in 628 B.C.

2 Chronicles 34:3 *For in the eighth year of his reign, while he was yet a boy, he began to seek the God of David his father, and in the twelfth year he began to purge Judah and Jerusalem of the high places, the Asherim, and the carved and the metal images.*

In 622 B.C., when Josiah was having the temple cleansed and repaired, Hilkiah, the high priest, found the book of the law. The book was read in Josiah's presence, and he was greatly humbled and convicted. Josiah led the people in covenant renewal, pledging himself and the people to serve God with a whole heart.

2 Chronicles 34:29 *Then the king sent and gathered together all the elders of Judah and Jerusalem. ³⁰ And the king went up to the house of the LORD, with all the men of Judah and the inhabitants of Jerusalem and the priests and the Levites, all the people both great and small. And he read in their hearing all the words of the Book of the Covenant that had been found in the house of the LORD. ³¹ And the king stood in his place and made a covenant before the LORD, to walk after the LORD and to keep his commandments and his testimonies and his statutes, with all his heart and all his soul, to perform the words of the covenant that were written in this book. ³² Then he made all who were present in Jerusalem and in Benjamin join in it. And the inhabitants of Jerusalem* *did according to the covenant of God, the God of their fathers. ³⁵ And Josiah took away all the abominations from all the territory that belonged to the people of Israel and made all who were present in Israel serve the LORD their God. All his days they did not turn away from following the LORD, the God of their fathers.*

Later, Josiah led them in a Passover observance, the first one like it since the days of Samuel, some 400 years earlier. This was a spectacular event, with thousands of animals—a time of hopefulness and a time of reform. It was during Josiah's reign that **the word of the LORD came to the prophet Zephaniah.**

THE MAN ZEPHANIAH (1:1)

We don't know much about this man, but the reference to his genealogy is unlike what we see for the other prophets. Zephaniah's introduction takes us back to his great-great grandfather, Hezekiah. We cannot be certain, but it may well be that this is King Hezekiah. If so, then Zephaniah is a prophet from royal descent and is a distant relative of Josiah. Zephaniah may thus have some access to the royal court, giving him an up-close view of some of the nation's sins. We also know that Zephaniah is faithful to deliver the word that God gives him.

THE MINISTRY OF ZEPHANIAH (1:1)

The date debate

His ministry takes place during the 31 years when Josiah is king. This makes him a contemporary of Jeremiah, whose ministry began somewhere around 627 B.C. and continued into the time when Judah fell to Babylon.

The major question about Zephaniah's ministry is whether his ministry is prior to Josiah's reforms of 628 and 622, or after. Those who argue for these messages being given <u>before</u> the reforms point out that he really doesn't reference the reforms in these oracles. They say this book is the warning from God that may have led to the reforms.

Those who argue for his messages being delivered <u>after</u> the reforms point out that even after the reforms, Jeremiah speaks of the sins of the people in the very same way. In addition, there are references in Zephaniah to the book of Deuteronomy, and those may indicate that the book of the law has already been discovered and has an influence on his message. Also, the reference to *the king's* (Josiah's) *sons in foreign attire* (1:8) suggests that Josiah is older and that they are old enough to make their own decisions. This argument also points out the reference to the *remnant of Baal* in verse 4, saying that this is what remains after the reforms have already begun.

TWO THINGS OF WHICH WE CAN BE CERTAIN

This message is given before Nineveh is destroyed.

2:13 *And he will stretch out his hand against the north and destroy Assyria, and he will make Nineveh a desolation, a dry waste like the desert.* ¹⁴ *Herds shall lie down in her midst, all kinds of beasts; even the owl and the hedgehog shall lodge in her capitals; a voice shall hoot in the window; devastation will be on the threshold; for her cedar work will be laid bare.* ¹⁵ *This is the exultant city that lived securely, that said in her heart, "I am, and there is no one else." What a desolation she has become, a lair for wild beasts! Everyone who passes by her hisses and shakes his fist.*

This places his message before the destruction of Nineveh in 612 B.C.

This message speaks to the superficial and temporary nature of the reforms.

Some say Zephaniah's ministry is before the reforms took place and likely has an impact on Josiah and the reforms that follow. Whether or not that is true, the reforms don't last beyond Josiah's reign. His son Jehoahaz reigns 3 months, doing what is evil in the sight of God. Then Jehoahaz is taken to Egypt, and his brother Jehoiakim is put in his place. Jehoiakim rules for 11 years, and he, too, does what is evil in the sight of the Lord. The Bible makes clear in 2 Chronicles 36 that the people sinned right along with them. Read what the prophet Jeremiah writes. This takes place just a few months after Josiah's death.

Jeremiah 26:1 *In the beginning of the reign of Jehoiakim the son of Josiah, king of Judah, this word came from the LORD:* ² *"Thus says the LORD: Stand in the court of the LORD's house, and speak to all the cities of Judah that come to worship in the house of the LORD all the words that I command you to speak to them; do not hold back a word.* ³ *It may be they will listen, and every one turn from his evil way, that I may relent of the disaster that I intend to do to them because of their evil deeds.* ⁴ *You shall say to them, 'Thus says the LORD: If you will not listen to me, to walk in my law that I have set before you,* ⁵ *and to listen to the words of my servants the prophets whom I send to you urgently, though you have not listened,* ⁶ *then I will make this house like Shiloh, and I will make this city a curse for all the nations of the earth.'"* ⁷ *The priests and the prophets and all the people heard Jeremiah speaking these words in the house of the LORD.* ⁸ *And* *when Jeremiah had finished speaking all that the LORD had commanded him to speak to all the people, then the priests and the prophets and all the people laid hold of him, saying, "You shall die!"*

Whether Zephaniah preaches before the reforms or after the reforms, it becomes plain that the reforms say more about Josiah's heart, than the people's hearts.

Huldah, the prophetess, makes this plain when she is consulted after the book of the law is found. She says disaster will certainly come upon Judah, but that Josiah will not live to see it happen.

2 Kings 22:18 *But to the king of Judah, who sent you to inquire of the LORD, thus shall you say to him, Thus says the LORD, the God of Israel: Regarding the words that you have heard, ¹⁹ because your heart was penitent, and you humbled yourself before the LORD, when you heard how I spoke against this place and against its inhabitants, that they should become a desolation and a curse, and you have torn your clothes and wept before me, I also have heard you, declares the LORD. ²⁰ Therefore, behold, I will gather you to your fathers, and you shall be gathered to your grave in peace, and your eyes shall not see all the disaster that I will bring upon this place."' And they brought back word to the king.*

THE MESSAGE OF ZEPHANIAH (BRIEFLY)

- The day of the Lord's judgment against Judah (1:2-2:3)
- The day of the Lord's judgments against the nations (2:4-3:8)

  The above two points apply both in the present and in the future. When God turns His judgment against the world, Jerusalem won't be spared.

- The day of the Lord's salvation (3:9-20)

  It will be worldwide, including a humble remnant in Judah.

We can think of Zephaniah's message this way:

- LOOK WITHIN the land of Judah – Judgment
- LOOK AROUND to the surrounding nations – Judgment

- LOOK BEYOND to a future time – Salvation of a humble remnant[1]

APPLICATION

We must recognize the difference between reform and repentance.

Reform occurs because of outward pressure and temporal motivations. In the case of Judah, there is the pressure of the possibility of reuniting the northern and southern kingdoms and the spiritual blessing that may come as a result.

Repentance occurs because of a heart-change wrought by God. Observe the Holy Spirit's work in Josiah's heart.

We must recognize the sad limits of reform.

Reforms don't last. Even if they lasted a lifetime, reforms don't save. Genuine love for God cannot be passed on by external means. **God transforms the heart.**

We must care about genuine repentance.

The need is not for us to exert pressure that may bring about some sort of external change that drives the real problem below the surface. We must pray and share the Word of God in view of the Lord's changing of people's hearts. If anything less happens, it cannot be saving in nature.

It is worth noting that Josiah was not wrong to lead in the reformation, paying attention to righteous standards. Nations tend to swing like a pendulum, from one end to the other. When things swing in a direction that seems more moral, there is celebration, as if politics is the answer for a people. Politics cannot save; only an outpouring of the Holy Spirit can save.

Genuine repentance in the lives of others

Entire nations won't be saved at once, just one soul at a time. There

---

[1] The three headings, "Look within, Look around, Look beyond," are from J. Sidlow Baxter, *Explore the Book.*

won't be worldwide salvation, a worldwide kingdom, until Jesus comes again. Work and pray for the salvation of individuals. As you teach your children and minister to the people you come in contact with, are you thinking and praying in those terms? Are you aiming not at reform, but at repentance?

Genuine repentance in our own lives

We should each be concerned about repentance, not only in the lives of others, but in our own life as well. Have you ever reformed instead of repented? You've agreed, adopted the standard and done what others expect of you, however, in your heart, you have remained unchanged. This contrasts with the times when the Lord has touched your heart so that no one had to say a word—you were ready to obey Him whatever it meant, whatever it took. Do you know the difference?

We must recognize signs of genuine repentance.

We get a picture of true repentance in Paul's second letter to the Corinthians.

2 Corinthians 7:8 *For even if I made you grieve with my letter, I do not regret it— though I did regret it, for I see that that letter grieved you, though only for a while. 9 As it is, I rejoice, not because you were grieved, but because you were grieved into repenting. For you felt a godly grief, so that you suffered no loss through us. 10 For godly grief produces a repentance that leads to salvation without regret, whereas worldly grief produces death. 11 For see what earnestness this godly grief has produced in you, but also what eagerness to clear yourselves, what indignation, what fear, what longing, what zeal, what punishment! At every point you have proved yourselves innocent in the matter.*

- True repentance is grieved by godly admonition, not angered; their heart is broken. (:8)
- True repentance does not stop at the point of grief. It leads to a change of mind and a change of heart that results in a change of course. (:9)
- True repentance leads to salvation, not to sin and death. (:10) There are two kinds of sorrow in the world regarding sin, godly sorrow and worldly sorrow. Worldly sorrow is fleshly and natural, leading to more sin eventually, including sin in the way you respond to sin. The outcome is destruction and death. Godly sorrow is supernatural, the product of the Holy Spirit's work in a heart, leading one to Christ. It leads to God, seeking His forgiveness, receiving it and pursuing Him in obedience.

- <u>True repentance longs for holiness</u>, not for a return to sin (:10 – *without regret*). See sin through the eyes of God, and you'll despise it, hate it and recognize the danger of it.
- <u>True repentance does not defend its wrong</u>. It's ready to demonstrate a new course (:11 – *indignation, fear, desire, zeal*, just *punishment*). It produces earnestness, eagerly wanting to clear oneself. There's a sense of anger at one's own failures. This anger is directed toward self, yet not in a way that leads to death, but leading to Christ. In the words of David, *Against you and you only I've sinned*. Now there is a reverence for God and a sense of holy fear!

There was a man named Josiah who wanted to follow the Lord. The Lord took hold of his heart as a 16-year-old young man, and he led an entire nation in righteous reforms. In his heart, it was real, but sadly, in the life of the nation, it was just reform. It wouldn't be long before they forgot those reforms and they were destroyed.

Repentance, not reformation, is the lesson of Zephaniah.

2
JUDGMENT NOW AND JUDGMENT TO COME
(1:2-13)

As we noted in the previous chapter, Zephaniah is ministering sometime between 640 B.C.-612 B.C., prior to the fall of Nineveh, during the reign of Josiah. He is writing around the time of the national reforms led by Josiah which were meant to remove idolatry and call the nation back to covenant faithfulness toward Yahweh. And yet that renewal would prove to be temporary. As a result, the southern kingdom of Judah would fall to Babylon in 586 B.C., just 23 years after Josiah died in 609.

Throughout history, the judgments of God against sin have also served as a preview of the future. Today they continue to speak of the judgment of the final day. By bringing judgments against sin, God warns everyone who witnesses those judgments to flee from the wrath that will come at the end of history.

This is not only true when events in this world are unmistakably the result of God's direct judgments. He graciously warns even through sudden tragedy, natural disasters, and what man would call "accidents." These things are full of lessons from God and point to the future.

Luke 13:1 *There were some present at that very time who told him about the Galileans whose blood Pilate had mingled with their sacrifices.* *2 And he answered them, "Do you think that these Galileans were worse sinners than all the other Galileans, because they*

suffered in this way? ³ *No, I tell you; but unless you repent, you will all likewise perish.*
⁴ *Or those eighteen on whom the tower in Siloam fell and killed them: do you think that
they were worse offenders than all the others who lived in Jerusalem?* ⁵ *No, I tell you; but
unless you repent, you will all likewise perish."*

Jesus makes the point that what happened to those people was not so
much a commentary on their own personal sinfulness, as on the general
sinfulness of mankind. Apart from God's forgiveness for our sins, everyone
will perish.

In the book of Zephaniah, we find warnings about the **Day of the Lord**.
It is the day of reckoning, when the sins committed come back upon the
heads of those who would not repent of them. Their sins return to them in
the form of judgment.

Obadiah 1:15 *For the day of the* LORD *is near upon all the nations. As you have
done, it shall be done to you; your deeds shall return on your own head.*

The *day of the* LORD is a major theme in the book of Zephaniah. When
you look at the many ways that Zephaniah refers to it, they even supersede
the multiple references found in the book of Joel. There are at least nineteen,
including *the day of the* LORD, *that day, a day,* and *the great day.* Beginning with
the second verse of the 1ˢᵗ chapter, down to the third verse of the 2ⁿᵈ chapter,
he announces a judgment of utter devastation. It is a judgment that calls for
silence and begs for repentance. God has raised up Zephaniah to warn of
that judgment and of an even greater judgment at the last day.

In this book there are four elements of a prophet's message: (1) an
announcement of the wrath of God, (2) an explanation of why that wrath is
coming, (3) a description of the nature of that wrath and (4) and a call to
repentance. Each of these four elements is found in this first section.

THE ANNOUNCEMENT OF GOD'S WRATH

Zephaniah announces the judgment of God. Judah is the focus in this
section, but the announcement begins by pointing us to worldwide
destruction.

Worldwide destruction (1:2-3, 17, 18)

He uses language that calls to mind the worldwide flood at the time of
Noah. It almost seems to describe the un-creation of the world. Looking at

day 5 and day 6 of creation, you see fish, birds, beasts, and man. As the Lord through Zephaniah declares what he will do, notice that he begins with *man,* then *beast, birds,* and *fish.* Man was the last, the crowning work of creation, but here man is the first to be described in this destruction. A destruction even greater than the flood is coming. Even the fish will be destroyed. (1:3)

Genesis 6:7 *So the LORD said, "I will blot out man whom I have created from the face of the land, man and animals and creeping things and birds of the heavens, for I am sorry that I have made them."*

Jeremiah, who prophesied around the same time as Zephaniah, had a similar warning from God.

Jeremiah 25:31 *The clamor will resound to the ends of the earth, for the LORD has an indictment against the nations; he is entering into judgment with all flesh, and the wicked he will put to the sword, declares the LORD.' * *32 "Thus says the LORD of hosts: Behold, disaster is going forth from nation to nation, and a great tempest is stirring from the farthest parts of the earth! * *33 "And those pierced by the LORD on that day shall extend from one end of the earth to the other. They shall not be lamented, or gathered, or buried; they shall be dung on the surface of the ground.*

Utter destruction (1:2-3, 18)

There are places in this first chapter when it clearly seems that what God is describing is a judgment that no one survives. Not only will mankind be destroyed, but even the ruins will be swept away. It will be thorough. Nothing will be left that offends the Lord God.

Judah's destruction (1:4)

While God describes here a judgment that is worldwide and complete, He also describes a judgment that is specifically coming upon Judah (1:4). This description enables us to determine that it historically occurred at the time when Judah fell to Babylon. He uses local terms, addressing the very specific sins of the nation at that time.

How do we explain this language that is worldwide and complete, yet local, and brought about by Babylon? One way is to understand the worldwide language to be hyperbolic, a way for the prophet to say that the judgment upon Judah will be complete. The better explanation, though, is that the judgment coming upon Judah serves as a type,[2] a warning of a more complete judgment arriving in a future day. God's wrath is coming, and the nation should be warned about a judgment that is near, but every individual who hears these words should also be concerned about the judgment that is final and ultimate.

ZEPHANIAH'S MESSAGE TO US

We must realize the same. In our own day we witness judgments; nations rise and fall, regimes come and go. Things happen in a few days that some people never dreamed could come to pass. But this turmoil simply points to the fact that all earthly kingdoms are temporary. They will all come tumbling down when Jesus establishes His kingdom. In some sense, we might say that the judgments of God known in the present day will reach their climax and conclusion on that great day.

THE EXPLANATION FOR GOD'S WRATH

God's anger toward Judah can be explained in more than one way. In general, they have been unfaithful to God. Despite His goodness, His patience, and all the ways that He's made Himself known to them, they have forsaken the Lord. And God hates that. They have violated the terms of the gracious covenant He made with them, and therefore suffer the curses of that covenant. We can say more than that because God's prophet, Zephaniah, names specific sins He will punish.

The Lord reveals five areas in which He will bring judgment. These are things that God hates—both in Zephaniah's day and now. Notice in this prophecy where the judgment of God's hand (:4) will reach.

God will judge in the realm of religion (1:4-7)

He begins with their worship. This is the stream from which all their sins flow.

The pagan priest (1:4) (The Hebrew word translated *idolatrous priests* is a word for an idol priest, a pagan priest.)

---

[2] In Biblical studies, a *type* is a person or a thing or an event that pre-figures some future person, thing or event in God's salvation plan.

We learn from the Old Testament that the kings of Judah have appointed non-Levitical priests to make offerings to false gods on the high places. There is worship of heavenly bodies, the sun, the moon, and the stars. For that, they'd want high places with a clear view. That is why he mentions going up on *roofs* and looking to *the host of the heavens.* There is the worship of the Canaanite fertility god called Baal and worship of Molech, the chief god of the Ammonites. Milcom is a Hebrew variation on the name Molech.

Why would the Lord's people fall into such idolatry?

- Sinful man is an idolater by nature, so that a wicked king would be drawn to such false worship.
- A king might do this for political purposes, to win favor with foreign leaders.
- From the standpoint of sinful superstition, a king might do this to gain military help.

Josiah's reforms sought to confront these kinds of behavior.

2 Kings 23:5 *And he deposed the priests whom the kings of Judah had ordained to make offerings in the high places at the cities of Judah and around Jerusalem; those also who burned incense to Baal, to the sun and the moon and the constellations and all the host of the heavens.*

The syncretistic priest (1:4b-5)

Some Levitical priests have compromised themselves. They try to mix the worship of Yahweh with idolatry—in this case, worshipping the heavenly bodies while calling upon Yahweh. They attempt to merge the worship of the false gods of the pagans with the worship of the true God.

Jeremiah 19:13 *The houses of Jerusalem and the houses of the kings of Judah—all the houses on whose roofs offerings have been offered to all the host of heaven, and drink offerings have been poured out to other gods—shall be defiled like the place of Topheth.*

God specifically warned His people about this.

Deuteronomy 4:19 *And beware lest you raise your eyes to heaven, and when you see the sun and the moon and the stars, all the host of heaven, you be drawn away and bow down to them and serve them, things that the LORD your God has allotted to all the peoples under the whole heaven.*

The various forms of false worship (1:6)

The Lord identifies idolatry, syncretism, and spiritual indifference as all worthy of His wrath. The second and third ones are especially important for us to hear in our culture. We have much mixed religion and may not see it as compromised worship, but it is. We say we love Jesus, but we don't love Him as much as our material things or our sinful desires. We think because there's no wooden idol or name of a false deity associated with what our culture runs after, we're not guilty of syncretism. But if you love the gods of this culture more than you love Christ, you are a compromised worshipper, and God hates it.

There are those who are living lives that are not overtly idolatrous, or even compromised, but who just have no real passion for God. We forget that the greatest commandment is a commandment about something <u>we are to do</u>.

Mark 12:30 *"You shall love the Lord your God with all your heart, all your mind, with all your soul, with all your strength."*

THE SACRIFICE OF GOD

God has prepared His own sacrifice and invited His own guests. God's name will be honored. His justice will be upheld. His holiness will be vindicated. The guests are the Babylonians, and the sacrifice is Judah.

God will judge in the realm of politics—leaders are not exempt (1:8)

The officials are those who served in the royal court. *The king's sons* apparently refers to the sons of Josiah who turned out to be wicked kings after him—Jehoahaz, Jehoiakim and Zedekiah.

These people are characterized by dressing in *foreign apparel*. Some have wondered if this is associated with the idolatry mentioned earlier, but the focus is probably on the fact that the apparel is *foreign*. Here are Israelites wanting to identify not with their own culture, but with a foreign culture. "Adopting foreign dress outwardly most likely implied that they also had absorbed foreign values and practices inwardly."[3]

---

[3]John F. Walvoord and Roy B. Zuck, eds., *The Bible Knowledge Commentary*. 2

External things matter beyond the most obvious matters of modesty and purity, because what goes on in our outward life speaks of the inclinations of our heart. Do we want to identify with our God? Do we desire to be distinctively godly?

There is nothing sinful about living in the culture you're in, unless you begin to embody the values of a wicked culture and display them by your desire to completely immerse yourself in them—your speech, relationships, pleasures, appearance and entertainment.

God will judge in the realm of social oppression—the powerful are not exempt (1:9)

It seems that now he is addressing those who plunder for material gain that they then devote, at least in part, to their false gods. Some have wondered if this is similar to an event that is mentioned in 1 Samuel, where the head and hands of the Philistines' pagan god were lying cut off on the threshold.

1 Samuel 5:1 *When the Philistines captured the ark of God, they brought it from Ebenezer to Ashdod. ² Then the Philistines took the ark of God and brought it into the house of Dagon and set it up beside Dagon. ³ And when the people of Ashdod rose early the next day, behold, Dagon had fallen face downward on the ground before the ark of the LORD. So they took Dagon and put him back in his place. ⁴ But when they rose early on the next morning, behold, Dagon had fallen face downward on the ground before the ark of the LORD, and the head of Dagon and both his hands were lying cut off on the threshold. Only the trunk of Dagon was left to him. ⁵ This is why the priests of Dagon and all who enter the house of Dagon do not tread on the threshold of Dagon in Ashdod to this day.*

However, the reference to violence and fraud in verse 9 may mean that they leap into the houses of others to take advantage of them. God cares about how we treat one another. In the context, He cares about social justice and hates injustice, oppression, violence and fraud.

God will judge in the realm of commerce (1:10-11)

God's judgment will fall on every part of the city of Jerusalem and on every part of Jewish society. In Zephaniah's day, the Fish Gate is in the

---

vols. Colorado Springs, CO: David C. Cook, 1989. "Zephaniah" chapter by John D. Hannah, p. 1527.

northern part of the city and the Second (or New) Quarter to the northwest of the temple area. The meaning of the hills is not clear. The crying, wailing and crashing is a vivid description of the scene yet to come.

The Mortar is the Hebrew הַמַּכְתֵּשׁ (*hammaktesh*). According to some sources, it's a market area, and the following statement seems to confirm that, as people are envisioned weighing out silver and trading. People are content with the making of money, but when God's judgment falls, their prosperity will end.

God will judge all foolish complacency (1:12-13)

The foolish contention (1:12)

Some foolishly say that the Lord will do nothing good or evil. They say in their heart that God doesn't care.

The fearful contrast (1:12)

Their contention contrasts with the reality that God is so real and so active that not a single person will escape. He pictures Himself as a lamp searching, and there will be no place to hide.

The frightening condition (1:12)

They are *complacent*. Literally, they *are thickening on the dregs*. The word *thickening* is translated from a word that literally means to "condense or to curdle." The analogy may relate to making wine. When the wine is fermenting, it can develop a hard crust. If the vessels are not being exchanged, the wine will be ruined. This pictures hearts that are stagnated and hard, no longer moved by the knowledge and truth of God.

The powerful consequences (1:13)

God will bring about a complete and irreversible destruction. They will not live long enough to rebuild.

APPLYING IT

1. Do we know that God's wrath is coming?
2. Do we know that God judges now and will judge finally?

17

3. Do we know what God hates?
   a. He judges in the realm of empty religion
   b. He judges in the realm of worldly politics
   c. He judges in the realm of oppressive violence
   d. He judges in the realm of business and making money
   e. He judges where men don't think his judgment is real
4. Do you know where to flee?

God's judgment is coming, so do you know where to hide? The Lord will search for you and drag you out. In Zephaniah 2:1-3, God tells you how to be hidden, but you dare not presume upon it. Do His just commands, seek righteousness and seek humility.

3
ONLY GOD CAN SAVE FROM GOD
(1:14-2:3)

We have already noted that Zephaniah speaks of judgments that are imminent and future. They will come upon Judah at the hands of the Babylonians, and upon the entire world. The judgments taking place throughout the history of the world are all types of the final judgment, and in some way, they belong to that final judgment. God's wrath is upon this world now, but its expression will reach a scope and power in the end unlike anything the world has seen before. James Montgomery Boice said it well: "As Judah was judged, so will we be judged. As they were warned, so are we."[4]

The Bible presents *the day of the Lord* in fearful terms. Sanity requires sobriety regarding that great day. At least 19 times in this book, the Holy Spirit of God, through Zephaniah, speaks of the day of the Lord in one way or another—and it's meant to awaken us. Other parts of the Scripture reinforce the point.

Psalm 90:11 *Who considers the power of your anger, and your wrath according to the fear of you?*

---

[4] James Montgomery Boice, *Minor Prophets* vol. 2 (Grand Rapids: Baker Books), 445.

Psalm 76:7 *But you, you are to be feared! Who can stand before you when once your anger is roused?*

Nahum 1:6 *Who can stand before his indignation? Who can endure the heat of his anger? His wrath is poured out like fire, and the rocks are broken into pieces by him.*

Jeremiah 10:10 *But the LORD is the true God; he is the living God and the everlasting King. At his wrath the earth quakes, and the nations cannot endure his indignation.*

Revelation 6:12 *When he opened the sixth seal, I looked, and behold, there was a great earthquake, and the sun became black as sackcloth, the full moon became like blood,* ¹³ *and the stars of the sky fell to the earth as the fig tree sheds its winter fruit when shaken by a gale.* ¹⁴ *The sky vanished like a scroll that is being rolled up, and every mountain and island was removed from its place.* ¹⁵ *Then the kings of the earth and the great ones and the generals and the rich and the powerful, and everyone, slave and free, hid themselves in the caves and among the rocks of the mountains,* ¹⁶ *calling to the mountains and rocks, "Fall on us and hide us from the face of him who is seated on the throne, and from the wrath of the Lamb,* ¹⁷ *for the great day of their wrath has come, and who can stand?"*

The Lord, through Zephaniah, is declaring judgment against Judah. He wants them to see that this judgment is due to their unfaithfulness to His covenant. The message of these verses is that **only God can save from God.** There is hope here, because He is compassionate, willing to forgive, if people repent and turn to Him.

THE DESCRIPTION OF GOD'S JUDGMENT (1:14-18)

The day of the Lord is approaching swiftly (1:14)

The word *near* comes first in the Hebrew text and is emphasized. They do not have much time, because the day of the Lord is near and quickly coming nearer. It is like a train barreling down upon a car stalled on the tracks, upon a people about to be devastated.

The day of the Lord is a day of great bitterness (1:14)

It is so near you can hear it: the sound of agony, defeat and hopelessness. The strong, valiant warrior cries out with despair as the bitterness of the day is tasted. It is a day of defeat, devastation, and great sorrow.

The day of the Lord is a day of multifaceted expressions of God's wrath (1:15-16)

There is a rhythmical organization to these statements. Kenneth L. Barker describes it well:

> **1:15** The next two verses continue the description of the day of the Lord as a day of defeat and ruin by employing six brief phrases without the use of a main verb. Each phrase begins with the word yôm, "day." "This passage [vv. 15–16a] is probably the most classical description of Yahweh's day in Israelite literature." Each yôm saying has a balanced (3 + 3) metrical structure. "Each saying has 7 syllables and the word ywm occurs 7 times. A complete stanza is thus formed."[5]

In English we don't get the complete sense of it. It is as though the horror of the day is meant to be impressed upon their minds in a chant, one description after another.

A day of wrath.
A day of distress and anguish (The Hebrew word for *wrath* sounds similar to the word for *distress*.)
A day of ruin and desolation (The Hebrew words for *ruin* and *desolation* sound similar.)
A day of darkness and gloom
A day of clouds and thick darkness (The Hebrew word for *clouds* starts with the same sound as the word for *thick darkness*.) This description is reminiscent of what the people of God had seen at Mount Sinai.

Deuteronomy 4:9 *"Only take care, and keep your soul diligently, lest you forget the things that your eyes have seen, and lest they depart from your heart all the days of your life. Make them known to your children and your children's children—* [10] *how on the day that you stood before the LORD your God at Horeb, the LORD said to me, 'Gather the people to me, that I may let them hear my words, so that they may learn to fear me all the days that they live on the earth, and that they may teach their children so.'* [11] *And you*

---

[5] Barker, K. L. (1999). *Vol. 20: Micah, Nahum, Habakkuk, Zephaniah*. The New American Commentary (439). Nashville: Broadman & Holman Publishers, and P. J. Nel as quoted by Barker.

came near and stood at the foot of the mountain, while the mountain burned with fire to the heart of heaven, wrapped in darkness, cloud, and gloom."

According to Moses, that appearance included a warning:

Deuteronomy 4:15-19 *"Therefore watch yourselves very carefully. Since you saw no form on the day that the LORD spoke to you at Horeb out of the midst of the fire, [16] beware lest you act corruptly by making a carved image for yourselves, in the form of any figure, the likeness of male or female, [17] the likeness of any animal that is on the earth, the likeness of any winged bird that flies in the air, [18] the likeness of anything that creeps on the ground, the likeness of any fish that is in the water under the earth. [19] And beware lest you raise your eyes to heaven, and when you see the sun and the moon and the stars, all the host of heaven, you be drawn away and bow down to them and serve them, things that the LORD your God has allotted to all the peoples under the whole heaven."*

The warning has to do with God's jealous judgment towards idolatry.

Deuteronomy 4:23-27 *Take care, lest you forget the covenant of the LORD your God, which he made with you, and make a carved image, the form of anything that the LORD your God has forbidden you. [24] For the LORD your God is a consuming fire, a jealous God. [25] "When you father children and children's children, and have grown old in the land, if you act corruptly by making a carved image in the form of anything, and by doing what is evil in the sight of the LORD your God, so as to provoke him to anger, [26] I call heaven and earth to witness against you today, that you will soon utterly perish from the land that you are going over the Jordan to possess. You will not live long in it, but will be utterly destroyed. [27] And the LORD will scatter you among the peoples, and you will be left few in number among the nations where the LORD will drive you."*

The darkness, gloom, and cloud that had spoken of God's presence in giving them His law, will now be present in the execution of His judgment because of the violation of that law. First came mercy, then judgment.

Jeremiah 13:16 *Give glory to the LORD your God before he brings darkness, before your feet stumble on the twilight mountains, and while you look for light he turns it into gloom and makes it deep darkness.*

Joel 2:1 *Blow a trumpet in Zion; sound an alarm on my holy mountain! Let all the inhabitants of the land tremble, for the day of the LORD is coming; it is near, [2] a day of darkness and gloom, a day of clouds and thick darkness! Like blackness there is spread upon the mountains a great and powerful people; their like has never been before, nor will be again after them through the years of all generations.*

While there may be physical tokens of what is spoken of here, including smoke that may block out the sun, or signs in the heavens, the ultimate meaning is that God is present in the judgment.

A day of trumpet blast and battle cry (1:16)
This will be a day of war. It will be especially bitter, because although this is a holy war, God is not battling for Judah, but against it. The Babylonians are only the instrument, and God is the great warrior, doing battle against sinful rebellion and unbelief.

The day of the Lord is inescapable (1:17-18)

The message now switches to the first person for emphasis. Judgment for Judah is inescapable, precisely because it is God's judgment. Verse 17 is constructed in a way that underscores the fact that this judgment is not arbitrary, but completely logical and just. It has the first two lines paired and the last two lines paired, with the middle statement standing alone prominently: *Because they have sinned against the Lord.* The shift to the first person shows the personal nature of our sin against God.

1. God will hem them in, (1:17a) The word for *distress* means to bind, to make narrow. They will feel closed in.
2. God will make it impossible for them to escape (1:17b) because they will be like *blind* men.
3. Their *blood* will be treated as worthless (17d), *like dust*. A similar comparison in the Psalms speaks of blood poured out *like water*.

Psalm 79 *A Psalm of Asaph.*
O God, the nations have come into your inheritance; they have defiled your holy temple; they have laid Jerusalem in ruins. [2] *They have given the bodies of your servants to the birds of the heavens for food, the flesh of your faithful to the beasts of the earth.* [3] *They have poured out their blood like water all around Jerusalem, and there was no one to bury them.*

4. *Their flesh* will be left to rot upon the ground. (1:17e) The word for *flesh* can refer to the intestines.
5. It is because *they have sinned against the Lord.* (1:17c) Sin is personal to God, because it is against HIM.
6. There will be nothing to save them.
   a. It is not what we think makes us safe. (1:16) Their *fortified cities* and *lofty battlements* will not do them any good.

b. It is not what we think buys us influence. (1:18) *Their silver* and *gold* will not do them any good. This is a jealous God at work. He is jealous for His honor, His name, and His holiness. He cannot be bribed.

We are again reminded that the judgment of Judah is just a part of what is coming upon the entire earth. Throughout the history of the world, all the judgments taking place come from God. They point to the fullest and greatest expression of His holy judgment and justice that will occur at the end of the age. The end of Zephaniah's description of judgment is devastating and should make us think about ourselves and our world.

THE ANSWER FOR GOD'S JUDGMENT (2:1-3)

The only hope for rescue from God's judgment is God. He alone is the only refuge.

The answer is repentance

Matthew Henry describes Zephaniah's message as intending "not to frighten them out of their wits, but to frighten them out of their sins."[6] Genuine repentance can be characterized in the following five ways:

1. It is not offended at its accurate description (2:1) – *Shameless nation.* There should be shame, sorrow and agreement with the assessment.
2. It believes God's warnings regarding the consequences of sin. (2:2)
3. It takes urgent action because judgment is coming. (2:2)
4. It does not just turn from sin; it turns to God (2:3) – *Seek* is a key word here. We are exhorted to seek righteousness and humility, and we can be hidden from the Lord's wrath The only refuge from the consuming wrath of God is God Himself.
5. It pursues a new course:
    *   A humble course, no longer a life of pride, but a life of submission to the authority of God.
    *   A heedful, obedient course that gives heed to carry out His commands.
    *   A holy, righteous course, one that desires what is right and pleasing in God's sight.

---

[6] Matthew Henry, Commentary on the Whole Bible in One Volume, p. 1168

- A humbly hopeful course. With humility of heart we can ask to be hidden from His wrath. We can seek Him, knowing that whatever we receive is just.

Finding God's mercy in Christ, we have a heart that is set on obedience to Him.

As Kenneth L. Barker noted, "Living in greater affluence and stronger defenses leads us to a greater feeling of security. We trust in the wealth we have accumulated or in the power of security devices, but the answer to the needs of our day is the same as that of Zephaniah's age—we must turn to God in humble submission. No other device or plan can save. The message is the same in every age. We must *seek the* LORD *and live* (Amos 5:6).[7]

---

[7] Barker, *Vol. 20: Micah, Nahum, Habakkuk, Zephaniah, 450.*

4
JUDGMENT ON THE NATIONS
(2:4-15)

Up to this point in the book of Zephaniah, except for the opening announcement of judgment, the focus has been on Judah. Now it expands to God's judgment upon the nations, specifically the peoples who surround Judah.

There are four pronouncements of judgment, each specifying the people who are the objects of God's wrath. Studies have revealed that this entire book may be viewed as one poem. It has a chiastic[8] structure, with verse 11 of chapter 2 standing in the center of the book, serving as its centerpiece as well as the centerpiece of these judgment announcements. Even though the word "kingdom" is not used, Almighty God is bringing about a worldwide kingdom in which all will be subject to Him and worship Him.

God groups the judgment pronouncements directionally, singling out the nations on the west, east, north and south. The peoples are addressed in some cases due to their proximity to Judah, and in some cases based upon a history with Judah—people near and far, nations small and great. The judgments are real, but there are also symbolic statements being made through them.

---

[8] A chiasm has ideas that go toward a center and then move out again in the opposite order, such as A, B, C, D, D, C, B, A.

JUDGMENTS UPON THE SURROUNDING NATIONS (2:4-15)

Judgment is coming to the west (2:4-7)

God begins with the seacoast region to the west of Judah, the land of the Philistines. Four of the five major Philistine cities are addressed, with Gath being the only one excluded. Some believe that Gath was already destroyed. *Cherethites* were a subgroup of Philistines and may have had historical connections to the island of Crete, because the name *Cherethites* relates to Crete.

The reference to being *driven out at noon* refers to either its surprising nature or its swiftness. There's an inscription on the Moabite Stone that speaks of a battle beginning prior to daylight, early in the morning, and ending by noon; the idea being a city that was easily taken. The devastation is total. It amounts to the depopulation of these areas. What were once cities will now be pastureland. Those who live there will be a *remnant* of God's people whom He preserves alive. In verse 7, what was once just held out as hope, is now held out in some measure, as a certainty.

Interspersed among the judgments we find the fulfillment of things the Lord promised in the Abrahamic covenant.

Genesis 12:1 *Now the LORD said to Abram, "Go from your country and your kindred and your father's house to the land that I will show you. ² And I will make of you a great nation, and I will bless you and make your name great, so that you will be a blessing. ³ I will bless those who bless you, and him who dishonors you I will curse, and in you all the families of the earth shall be blessed."*

Genesis 22:17 *"I will surely bless you, and I will surely multiply your offspring as the stars of heaven and as the sand that is on the seashore. And your offspring shall possess the gate of his enemies, ¹⁸ and in your offspring shall all the nations of the earth be blessed, because you have obeyed my voice."*

It is *the word of the Lord* that determines these things (2:5). When the Lord speaks, it always comes into being, and no one can withstand it. God is *mindful* of His people. Because of His care for His people, He will *restore their fortunes* (2:7).

Judgment is coming to the east (2:8-10)

Who are the Moabites and the Ammonites?

They are the descendants of Lot and his two daughters. After Lot's wife turned to salt, his daughters decided to have relations with him, so they could have descendants. One had a son named Moab, and the other, a son named Ben-Ammi, from which came the Moabites and Ammonites.[9] There was a long history of trouble from these people who had a blood kinship to the Israelites.

What is their sin?

Zephaniah told us nothing specific about the sins of Philistia. By contrast, for Moab and Ammon, two specific sins are mentioned: <u>Greed</u> for the land belonging to God's people and <u>pride</u>, which is reflected in their boasting against the land.

What will they receive?

- They will be destroyed.
- They will be plundered.
- Their land will be possessed by the remnant.
- They will get a return on their pride. There will be consequences. Pride always loses what it boasts about. Its confidence is always shown to be foolish.

Judgment is coming to the south (2:12)

The land of Cush refers to the upper region of the Nile. There was also a time of *Cushite* dominance in Egypt, so this could be a reference to Egypt. Cush was a son of Ham, who was a son of Noah, and Cush is where he settled.

> The "Cushites" referred to the people of the modern-day Sudan and Ethiopia. Zephaniah had now moved from west and east to south. At least three explanations could be given for why the prophet singled out the people of Cush. First, Zephaniah may have

---

[9] Genesis 19:23-38

chosen the Cushites as a known people who lived on the edge of the world. Therefore, the power of God reached to the very ends of the world. This is one of the powerful messages of the book and of the section concerning the judgment of the foreign nations: the Lord is not confined to the land of Judah and the people of Israel. He is the Lord of the whole world.

....at an earlier time, an Ethiopian dynasty ruled Egypt (Isa 18:1–2; 20:3–4). Zephaniah may have spoken the message of God against Egypt, Judah's powerful neighbor to the south. This interpretation would balance the prophecy since Assyria, Judah's powerful neighbor to the north, also received a message of condemnation. [10]

God's word of judgment to them is simple and clear: *You...shall be slain by my sword.*

Judgment is coming to the north (2:13-15)

God will take action on Assyria. As we have noted, in Zephaniah's day, Assyria is already dealing with some trouble, but Nineveh has not yet fallen. People still cannot imagine what will happen to Assyria very soon. Nineveh will be destroyed in 612 B.C., and Assyria will fall in 609.

Nineveh at that time is the most powerful city one could imagine. Its population in Jonah's day had been over 120,000.[11] There was an outer wall to the city and an inner wall that was 8 miles in circumference. Farming between the walls could provide them with all the food they needed.

The city was the world's largest. It had an inner city and an outer city, and these were probably augmented greatly by suburban development. The inner city was surrounded by a wall eight miles in circumference. It was 100 feet high and was so wide that three chariots could have raced around it abreast. It had twelve hundred towers and fourteen gates. Another mighty wall surrounded most of the outer city... Nearby (to the king's palace) was a 46-acre armory where the king kept his chariots,

[10] Barker, *Vol. 20: Micah, Nahum, Habakkuk, Zephania,* 463–464.

[11] Jonah 4:11

armor, horses and other military equipment. Nineveh was an awesome and seemingly impregnable metropolis. Yet it was overthrown suddenly and was left utterly desolate, as Zephaniah said."[12]

The description of the devastation is haunting and ironic. Nineveh was famous for a complex irrigation system, yet they will be left *a dry waste like the desert*. Historians tell us that one thing that played a huge role in the fall of the city was the unexpected flooding of the Tigris River. In dry season, there came a torrential downpour of rain and the river overran its banks. That contributed to the breaking down of the inner wall. Wild animals will now inhabit the buildings that were once reasons for pride

Two things are emphasized here.

1. This was a proud city.
2. This will be a mocked city. She thought she was impregnable, an exalted city that had nothing to fear, but she will become the object of jeering.

THE JUDGMENTS AND GOD'S ULTIMATE PURPOSE (2:11)

Standing in the middle of all of this is a reminder that there is a larger purpose at work. God has determined a kingdom. He will bring about a world that submits to Him as God and King. That larger purpose is associated with gracious covenants that He has made, covenants that impact the entire earth.

A. God made a covenant with **Abraham**. Those who have troubled Israel will be troubled.
B. God made a covenant through **Moses**. This is why God's people are called to faithfulness. Their sins will be punished, and God will restore them.
C. God made a covenant with **David**. This is the reason that they will possess their land and have their king on the throne (3:15).
D. God made a covenant with **Noah**. The world will not be destroyed by flood, and we see a picture of the world destroyed by fire.
E. God made a **new covenant** that involves the outpouring of salvation. That day is spoken of in the latter part of verse 11—*to him*

---

[12] Boice, *Minor Prophets*, 450-451.

[that is, to the Lord] *shall bow down, each in its place, all the lands of the nations.*

God's word is sure, and His promises will come to pass.

TIMELESS LESSONS FROM THESE JUDGMENT PRONOUNCEMENTS

A. God is **sovereign**—He rules the nations, and His word determines the future.

B. God **remembers and judges**—He is able to call to mind the sins committed in the past, including things spoken, and justice will be done.

C. God is **just and equitable**—The judgments match the offences, the chief of which is pride.

D. God will be **glorified**—His glory is the end for which He created the world and all things.

This has a practical bearing upon our lives.

- How will God be glorified? In his Son.
- By whom will God be glorified? By every man, woman and child, either through salvation or judgment.
- Where will God be glorified? In every realm – including the earth.
- Who or what can prevent God being glorified? No one, nothing!

5
ON THE BRINK OF RUIN
(3:1-8)

One of the questions we should ask when we study the Bible is, "What truth is taught in this passage about God?" The Bible is a God-centered book. We often go to it looking for answers for our lives, and that's right, but we need to remember that it's a book about God. It reveals the true God to us. He is revealed by the descriptions given of Him, by the things said by Him, by the commandments from Him, and by the great deeds accomplished by Him.

We have just finished a section in which God has foretold the judgment of all of Israel's enemies. West, east, south and north, the enemies of Israel will be judged. We can imagine Zephaniah's original audience nodding their heads in approval as the Lord pronounces judgment against the wicked city of Nineveh (2:15). But what follows must have shocked them. He pivots from describing the wicked city of Nineveh, to describing the wicked city of Jerusalem. We know that it's Jerusalem, because he says *She does not trust in the LORD; she does not draw near to her God* (3:2). In 3:14, he makes it even more explicit, referring to *Zion*.

GOD ANNOUNCES JUDGMENT ON THE CITY KNOWN BY HIS NAME.

Zephaniah is ministering during the reign of King Josiah. The book of 2 Kings gives us background.

2 Kings 23:24 *Moreover, Josiah put away the mediums and the necromancers and the household gods and the idols and all the abominations that were seen in the land of Judah and in Jerusalem, that he might establish the words of the law that were written in the book that Hilkiah the priest found in the house of the* LORD. *²⁵ Before him there was no king like him, who turned to the* LORD *with all his heart and with all his soul and with all his might, according to all the Law of Moses, nor did any like him arise after him. ²⁶ Still the* LORD *did not turn from the burning of his great wrath, by which his anger was kindled against Judah, because of all the provocations with which Manasseh had provoked him. ²⁷ And the* LORD *said, "I will remove Judah also out of my sight, as I have removed Israel, and I will cast off this city that I have chosen, Jerusalem, and the house of which I said, My name shall be there."*

What truth about God is found here in Zephaniah 3 and also in 2 Kings? **God hates sin wherever He finds it.** God judges sin without respect of persons. When God has been merciful and gracious to you, it does not set you free to sin! It makes you even more responsible for your sin. The fact that Jerusalem is the city associated with His name does not mean that they will be spared when He judges sin.

God's people are not to continue in their sin—they are to repent and forsake it. God often gives space for repentance, but when that grace is not responded to with repentance, then all that is left is judgment.

In this chapter, we will see four evidences that holy God is faithful to judge sins as they deserve to be judged. **But as we look at these evidences, let us not be like Judah. Let us not imagine that we can ignore our own sins and think that God only hates sin in others.** Let us judge (rightly discern) our own sins so that God has no need to discipline us for those sins. It's better to respond to the voice of God than to have to encounter the rod of God. Remember what God said through the apostle Paul.

1 Corinthians 11:28 *Let a person examine himself, then, and so eat of the bread and drink of the cup. ²⁹ For anyone who eats and drinks without discerning the body eats and drinks judgment on himself. ³⁰ That is why many of you are weak and ill, and some have died. ³¹ But if we judged ourselves truly, we would not be judged. ³² But when we are judged by the Lord, we are disciplined so that we may not be condemned along with the world.*

So, as we examine ourselves, wherever our merciful God reveals our sins to us, let us acknowledge those sins and repent of them, because God hates sin wherever He finds it, and He deals with sin without respect of persons.

A SUMMARY OF SINS THAT DESERVE GOD'S JUDGMENT (3:1)

Verse 1 is an announcement of judgment with a summary of the charges. Zephaniah begins by announcing the sinful character of the city of Jerusalem. This general summary also seems to have a logical order in the Hebrew text. She is **rebellious, defiled** and **oppressing**. Zephaniah is showing the very nature of sin. The word *rebellious* speaks of the city's attitude toward God. *Defiled* speaks of the condition of her own life. *Oppressing* speaks of her treatment of people. And this is the way that it always goes. What we are toward God determines who we are, and who we are determines how we treat others. As Kenneth Barker says, "the Hebrew order of these words serves to illustrate the way sin works. Sin is *rebellion* against God that *pollutes* or *defiles* the very being of the sinner, who then strikes out by *oppressing* others."[13] If Barker is right, then their character toward God, self and others is on display. "True society arises from committed obedience (not rebellion) and from personal holiness (not defilement)."[14] If we want our relationships to be healthy, it all begins with our relationship to God. Obedience to God combined with personal holiness is what transforms how we deal with others.

MANIFESTATIONS OF THE SINS THAT DESERVE GOD'S JUDGMENT (3:2-5)

God, through Zephaniah, now becomes more specific. Sin is not some indistinct, indefinable thing, and it's not defined by us. It is concrete, demonstrated through specific acts and in specific relationships, and it's defined by God, determined by His word. Even when it exists in the realm of thoughts and attitudes, those thoughts and attitudes can be recognized as sin in the light of God's word. That's why merely denying that we're in sin doesn't mean that we're not in sin.

She's in rebellion against God (3:2)

---

[13] Barker, *Vol. 20: Micah, Nahum, Habakkuk, Zephaniah,* 474.

[14] Barker, *Vol. 20: Micah, Nahum, Habakkuk, Zephaniah,* 475.

Zephaniah mentions four ways that Jerusalem's rebellion against God is being manifested. Incidentally, rebellion against God is still seen in these four ways. If you're rebelling against the Lord, these four things are showing up in your life.

By *not listening*

She listens to no voice. Zephaniah obviously has in mind that she will not listen to God. When people will not listen to God, they also reject the voices that represent God. In those days, they wouldn't hear the prophets like Zephaniah. Today, they won't listen to people who give them God's truth. They do not listen to sound counsel. If they hear it, they won't follow it. They are like a child who holds his ears in an effort not to hear the truth. This becomes a general character quality. There is a stubbornness that characterizes the life. Every covenant curse was directed against those who would not hear the voice of God (Deut 28:45, 62).[15] People who are rebellious against God are stubborn in the face of those voices that are speaking for God. Godly people are teachable people. They want light, so they listen to a godly voice—not just to hear, but to accept and to obey.

By *not yielding* to correction

She accepts no correction. Rebellion is not yielding to God's Word of correction, not yielding to His discipline and warnings. God's Word would give correction, but the stubborn city—and anyone rebelling against the Lord—does not want correction. She does not want discipline, and she won't heed warnings. This is a mark of a life on the wrong road. There is stubbornness in general, and specifically an unwillingness to be corrected with the truth of God.

By *not trusting* in Yahweh

What is the opposite of stubborn rebellion against the Lord? It's faith in God. The opposite of being in rebellion against God, not listening to Him, and not yielding to Him, is believing God.

Why would we not want to listen? Why would we not want to be corrected? Because we want to go our own way. We want to do it our own

---

[15] James E. Smith, *The Minor Prophets*, Old Testament Survey Series (Joplin, MO: College Press, 1994), Zep 3:2.

way. We think we know best. To obey God's Word would mean that we would have to acknowledge that we're on the wrong path. To believe God means I don't believe me, and I don't believe any voice that's the opposite of what His Word says. It means I'm going to believe Him. It means I'm willing to obey Him, relinquishing control of my life to God, even when it means correction for my life.

We are often unwilling to see our problem for what it really is. Why are we so stubborn? Why are we resistant toward the people who can really help us with God's word? Why are we unwilling to hear what we don't want to hear? We are often stubborn and unwilling to be corrected because the word of God demands our faith in God. A self-driven life is a faithless life. Our problem is a faith problem. In faith, you submit. In faith, it isn't your way, it's God's way. In faith, Scripture is the standard.

An unwillingness to believe God is not an amoral act. We may recognize that sexual sin, for example, is immoral, but refusing to believe God is also immoral. It is great wickedness. It's at the root of every other sin. And faithlessness is not without consequence.

Hebrews 3:15 *As it is said, "Today, if you hear his voice, do not harden your hearts as in the rebellion." 16 For who were those who heard and yet rebelled? Was it not all those who left Egypt led by Moses? 17 And with whom was he provoked for forty years? Was it not with those who sinned, whose bodies fell in the wilderness? 18 And to whom did he swear that they would not enter his rest, but to those who were disobedient? 19 So we see that they were unable to enter because of unbelief.*

This is a city on the brink of ruin, and what characterizes the city is its unwillingness to trust in Yahweh.

By *not drawing near* to God

She does not draw near to her God. This is another way of saying she doesn't truly worship Him. James E. Smith comments,

What a bold accusation to make against a city where morning and evening sacrifices were offered each day in the temple of Yahweh! To draw near to God requires faith, a contrite heart, loving gratitude, and exclusive devotion. Truly drawing near to

Yahweh excludes any dalliance with other deities. On all counts Jerusalem failed. The place was devoid of true worship (3:2).[16]

<u>When these other things are going on, there is no true worship taking place</u>. If we go through the motions of worship, but don't listen to God, if we don't yield to Him and don't trust Him, all our worship is an unacceptable sham. If we do that, expressing worship to God only outwardly, we walk in the footsteps of this city, a city on the brink of ruin.

An evidence that someone is not listening, yielding and trusting is that the person does not draw near to God. Faith draws near to God. But when we don't believe God, and we don't want to be confronted with our lack of faith in Him, we run from the light.

Her leaders oppress people (3:3)

Rebellion is not Jerusalem's only sin. Because this city is rebellious, it is also characterized by oppression. The oppressive nature of this city is seen in her leaders. Her civil officials, who determine cases, should be protecting the innocent. Instead, they are devouring the people. Like roaring lions and ravenous wolves, they devour people and leave nothing but poverty and oppression.

The city's leaders are preying upon the people that they are supposed to care for; taking advantage of those whom they should shepherd and for whom they should execute justice. They take advantage of the poor and the helpless. They find their victims wherever they can.

This is what can happen in a nation, a city or a home. The further we move from the fear of the Lord, the more we lose the best motive for the right treatment of people. Eventually, the result is chaos. Why should we treat people with justice and righteousness? Because there is a living God to whom we must give account. Always remember that God is not just concerned about sins directly against Him, but also those sins that are against people.

I am amazed at the blindness that exists in my nation.

---

[16] James E. Smith, *The Minor Prophets*, Zep 3:2.

- We treat sexual sin as if it isn't a sin against anyone but ourselves—forgetting that it's a sin against everyone who is impacted by it.
- We treat marriage as a mere contract, and we forget that divorce is breaking a vow that God has witnessed.
- We celebrate the murder of babies in the womb, ignoring the violence of it.
- We take advantage of people in the realm of business, deceiving and cheating and stealing just to make money.
- Parents abandon their children.
- Children grow up to abandon their parents.
- We sin against others by our speech, especially online.

Do we think God will simply overlook these sins?

Her religion is defiled (3:4)

Yet another aspect of Jerusalem's sinful condition is the defiling presence of false religion. When God is not heeded because He is not believed, and when that is being manifested by oppressive treatment of other people, then the only kind of "worship" toward God is that which is defiled and offensive toward Him. Religion becomes a mockery.

1. *Fickle* and *treacherous* prophets – The word translated *fickle* may mean insolent and reckless. The prophets are not honorable men, not men of dignity. They do not display fear of the Lord. They are rude and unpredictable. And they are *treacherous*, the word meaning to be faithless or disloyal. The prophets are undisciplined, unreliable, deceitful, untrustworthy men. Why? Because they don't trust the Lord; they don't fear the Lord. The fear of the Lord is what makes a man careful in ministry. By contrast, these men don't have true fear of the Lord, so they do what seems best to them, and they are completely unreliable as a result.

2. *Profane* priests – They *profane what is holy*. They treat holy things in a way that reflects no fear of the Lord, defiling them. *They do violence to the law.* This seems to indicate a boldfaced disregard for God's laws.

What is this? It is apostate religion led by apostate guides.

Do you think your religious involvement and your religious activity is pleasing to God while you refuse to believe Him and to honor Him by the way you treat others? If you do, then you walk in the footsteps of this kind of religion and these kinds of men.

Her guilt is shown by God's faithfulness (3:5)

What makes all of this even more heinous, and completely without excuse, is that God remains faithful all along. The God whom Jerusalem worships (at least in name), the God who has been involved with her from her inception, is righteous, just and faithful. To be ashamed, all that she must do is look at herself against the backdrop of her God's character. And yet this city *knows no shame*. A question for each of us is, <u>Does God's character ever make me ashamed of my own</u>? If it doesn't, that's not a good thing. Looking into the face of our God's righteous and just and faithful character should transform our own character:

- He is righteous, and I want to be righteous.
- He is just, and I want to treat others with justice.
- He is faithful, and I want to be faithful.

We must confess our sins and our rebellion. We've all been defiled. We were born into this world estranged from God. We have rebelled. Yet there is life in Jesus. God has provided all that we need.

- Will you listen to Him?
- Will you yield to Him?
- Will you believe Him?
- Will you draw near to Him?
- Will you repent of any mistreatment of others?
- Will you bow before Him and draw near with a true and honest heart? Will you make your religion genuine?
- Will you examine yourself in the light of God's perfect character?

> *The LORD within her is righteous;*
> *he does no injustice;*
> *every morning he shows forth his justice;*
> *each dawn he does not fail...*

- Will you let the knowledge of His character transform yours?

GOD'S DEALINGS WITH SINFUL MEN SHOULD LEAD US TO REPENTANCE (3:6-8)

Verse 6 continues what we have already seen, but in verse 6 there is a change. God begins to address the wicked city in the first person, speaking directly to her sinful condition. He reveals the justice and the certainty of the judgments coming upon her.

The <u>history</u> of God's dealings with sinful people should lead us to repentance (3:6)

I have cut off nations…I have laid waste their streets. There are no nations specified in the statements of verse 6. It cannot be the judgment of the nations just addressed in chapter 2, because those judgments are future. This is a general reference to how God deals with nations throughout history. It's what He had done to Judah's neighbor to the north (Israel) and it's what He's said in 1:2 that He will do in the future—*I will utterly sweep away everything from the face of the earth.* Shouldn't such statements raise them (and us) to a high alert level?

God has cut off nations

He has brought them down. The idea is to destroy. God Himself has destroyed nations. Scripture clearly teaches that what happens in history is the work of God. Nations rise, and nations fall, and it is God who does both.

Psalm 75:6 *For not from the east or from the west and not from the wilderness comes lifting up,* ⁷ *but it is God who executes judgment, putting down one and lifting up another.*

Nebuchadnezzar, the great ruler in Daniel's time, learned this.

Daniel 4:29 *At the end of twelve months he was walking on the roof of the royal palace of Babylon,* ³⁰ *and the king answered and said, "Is not this great Babylon, which I have built by my mighty power as a royal residence and for the glory of my majesty?"* ³¹ *While the words were still in the king's mouth, there fell a voice from heaven, "O King Nebuchadnezzar, to you it is spoken: The kingdom has departed from you,* ³² *and you shall be driven from among men, and your dwelling shall be with the beasts of the field. And you shall be made to eat grass like an ox, and seven periods of time shall pass over* *you, until you know that the Most High rules the kingdom of men and gives it to whom he will."*

If we ask what makes for the health and safety of nations, or what makes for the fall and destruction of nations, God gives us an answer.

Proverbs 14:34 *Righteousness exalts a nation, but sin is a reproach to any people.*

Proverbs 11:10 *When it goes well with the righteous, the city rejoices, and when the wicked perish there are shouts of gladness. ¹¹ By the blessing of the upright a city is exalted, but by the mouth of the wicked it is overthrown.*

These are principles of divine wisdom proven over and over again throughout human history.

History also proves that individual men, and societies of men, tend to think that they will be the exception. Sinful men feel confident in their sin. They can look back and see society after society (or individual life after individual life) torn apart by what God calls sin and unrighteousness and not really believe that they are in any danger. They usually feel this way because nothing bad has seemed to happen yet. "We still have money. We still have military power. We still have influence." They ignore God's warnings.

He has proven defenses to be defenseless.

Their battlements (literally their corners) *are in ruins.* Their populated places—*their streets, their cities*—are ghost towns *without a man, without an inhabitant.*

Knowing that this has happened again and again throughout history should cause any individual, city or nation to realize that there is no safety when we make ourselves the enemies of God. This should lead to repentance, faith in the true God, and submission to Him.

The <u>desire</u> present in God's dealings with sinful people should lead us to repentance (3:7)

I said, 'Surely you will fear me; you will accept correction. Then your dwelling would not be cut off according to all that I have appointed against you.

The Bible is clear that God is omniscient. He is not in the process of discovering things. So, when the Bible speaks to us as if God is discovering something, or is surprised by something, or is disappointed in His expectations, God is communicating with us in a way that we can relate to in our finiteness.

What is God communicating here? <u>There is a desire</u> (not an expectation) <u>in the heart of God that men would learn from his past judgments and escape</u> <u>from future judgments.</u> We can say it this way: God delights in mercy.

Ezekiel 18:32 *For I have no pleasure in the death of anyone, declares the Lord GOD; so turn, and live."*

Ezekiel 33:11 *Say to them, As I live, declares the Lord GOD, I have no pleasure in the death of the wicked, but that the wicked turn from his way and live; turn back, turn back from your evil ways, for why will you die, O house of Israel?*

Jonah understood this.

Jonah 4:2 *And he prayed to the LORD and said, "O LORD, is not this what I said when I was yet in my country? That is why I made haste to flee to Tarshish; for I knew that you are a gracious God and merciful, slow to anger and abounding in steadfast love, and relenting from disaster.*

Our God's nature and heart is that where men are willing to repent, He will relent, because He takes pleasure in mercy. That's what he's communicating in Zephaniah 3:7.

The truth that God delights in mercy will affect both how we preach His judgments and how we hear them. Sometimes, people preach His judgments as if He takes more delight in judgment than in mercy, but the true God magnifies His mercy and His grace. We must preach the judgment of God because it's certain, and we warn people to flee from it. Yet we should always make the way of escape plain because God is willing that men would turn and be forgiven.

God's mercy affects how we listen. Why does He warn us of judgment? So that there is the possibility and the opportunity for people to repent, to receive forgiveness in Christ and to escape His coming wrath. What makes His judgment especially terrible is that it follows so much mercy that was not heeded. God's judgments in times past should <u>instruct us</u> today.

- We should learn to fear Him. *Surely you will fear me.*
- We should learn to accept His correction. *Surely ... you will accept correction.*
- We should seek His mercy. *Then your dwelling would not be cut off.*
- Our desires should change. We should desire purity, not corruption. We should desire obedience, not sinful deeds. But what happened with Judah was just the opposite. The end of Zephaniah 3:7 literally says that they *rose early* to *make all their deeds corrupt.* They were so eager that they couldn't stay in bed. They were like a child at Christmas, up early, eager for what they delight in.

Do you recognize that something is desperately wrong in your soul when you have a strong desire for that which God fiercely hates? Do you recognize the foolishness and the danger of running after, with desire and eagerness, what God has already judged countless people for in the past?

Isaiah 59:1 *Behold, the* LORD's *hand is not shortened, that it cannot save, or his ear dull, that it cannot hear;* 2 *but your iniquities have made a separation between you and your God, and your sins have hidden his face from you so that he does not hear.* 3 *For your hands are defiled with blood and your fingers with iniquity; your lips have spoken lies; your tongue mutters wickedness.* 4 *No one enters suit justly; no one goes to law honestly; they rely on empty pleas, they speak lies, they conceive mischief and give birth to iniquity.* 5 *They hatch adders' eggs; they weave the spider's web; he who eats their eggs dies, and from one that is crushed a viper is hatched.* 6 *Their webs will not serve as clothing; men will not cover themselves with what they make. Their works are works of iniquity, and deeds of violence are in their hands.* 7 *Their feet run to evil, and they are swift to shed innocent blood; their thoughts are thoughts of iniquity; desolation and destruction are in their highways.* 8 *The way of peace they do not know, and there is no justice in their paths; they have made their roads crooked; no one who treads on them knows peace.* 9 *Therefore justice is far from us, and righteousness does not overtake us; we hope for light, and behold, darkness, and for brightness, but we walk in gloom.*

This is no theoretical behavior. Most of us have loved ones who know the truth, who have been taught the truth, but even more than that, have personally witnessed others destroyed by the very sins they now pursue. There is nothing new under the sun. Sin blinds people. This is what was happening in Judah. In light of the Lord's past dealings with people, they should have repented. Their desires should have been transformed. *But all the more they were eager to make all their deeds corrupt* (3:7).

The openness of God's dealings with sinful people should lead us to repentance (3:8)

"Therefore wait for me," declares the LORD... God is not making future judgment a secret. He's declaring it openly and plainly, giving everyone an opportunity to flee from the coming wrath. In verse 8, God seems to be speaking to a faithful remnant (see 2:1-3), to a humble, obedient people within a people.[17] Judgment is coming, but there is a remnant within the people who do not delight in the things that God hates. They are looking for the Lord to arise and to bring this to an end. In the midst of this sin-sick world, we're taught to pray for the Lord Jesus to come—and when He comes, He's bringing justice with Him.

Matthew 6:10 *Your kingdom come, your will be done, on earth as it is in heaven.*

God is saying to this remnant that all they have to do is wait and watch, because He is surely coming. Think about all that is on display in these words about the nature and character of God.

- God's wisdom is on display – He determines the time for judgment.
- God's faithfulness is on display – He is surely coming. He doesn't say to wait for "the day when I might rise up." He says to wait for *the day when I rise up.*
- God's patience is on display – there is still time to repent. (Why is He waiting?)
- God's omnipotence is on display – for when He arises, those to be judged are no more than *prey* for Him to seize.
- God's sovereignty is on display – *For My decision is to gather nations...* He has the right to decide. He will gather and assemble the nations for judgment. – He rules the whole world. The prophet Joel spoke similarly, prophesying the second coming of Christ.

Joel 3:1 *"For behold, in those days and at that time, when I restore the fortunes of Judah and Jerusalem,* [2] *I will gather all the nations and bring them down to the Valley of Jehoshaphat. And I will enter into judgment with them there, on behalf of my people and my heritage Israel, because they have scattered them among the nations and have divided*

---

[17] Some disagree with this interpretation. John Calvin believed He's saying, in effect, that the time of mercy has passed; now just wait for me in judgment.

up my land, ³ and have cast lots for my people, and have traded a boy for a prostitute, and have sold a girl for wine and have drunk it.

- God's <u>holiness</u> is on display – for His hatred for these sins is fierce, with *indignation* and *burning anger* and *fire* of *jealousy*. He's jealous for what is rightfully His: the honor and worship of all humanity. It's a frightening thought that this God who would rather show mercy than judge, when the appointed time of mercy is past, will be seen with burning anger and indignation. What makes the judgment of God all the more horrifying is the fact that so much mercy preceded it, and so many opportunities to repent, to be saved from the wrath that is coming. *But you would not* (Matthew 21:37).
- God's <u>authority</u> is on display – He owns the world and has the rights to its honor, so that His judgment can be spoken of as a jealousy in verse 8 – ... *In the fire of my jealousy all the earth shall be consumed.* He is jealous for what is rightfully His, the honor and worship of all humanity. What is rightfully His has not been given to God. Instead, He has been dishonored by rebellious men. Though He has been merciful and willing to forgive, they have chosen judgment instead.

You see, God has not been quiet about His judgment upon sin and sinners. No man can ever say truthfully that it catches him off guard, unless he hasn't been paying attention. God's plan, His decision to judge the world, is not something that He has hidden.

The OPENNESS of God with sinful humanity gives ample opportunity to flee from the wrath that is coming. But how does one flee from that wrath? How does one repent? Has God made a way for the world of humanity to find safety and refuge from His indignation, from His burning anger? Indeed, He has. God poured out His wrath for sin upon His own Son, so that all who turn from sin and who look to Him will be spared. Will you fear Him? Will you accept his correction? Will you turn from your sin so that you won't be judged? Will you urge others to do so? He is ready to be merciful, but He will judge fiercely.

6

THE PROMISE OF SALVATION
(3:9-13)

When Christ returns to the earth, He will bring judgment with Him. Throughout our study of Zephaniah, we have seen a great emphasis on judgment. The Lord, through Zephaniah, has just described a worldwide judgment in verses 1-8 of chapter 3. However, the book of Zephaniah does not end on the note of judgment. The God of sovereign grace ends it with the promise of a great salvation. In addition to being a time of judgment, the return of Christ will mean a world in which salvation is on display. The outpouring of God's salvation grace will be witnessed both in a saved Israel and in the worship of the true God among the nations. This is the pattern throughout the Minor Prophets. There's much pronouncement of judgment, but they always end on the note of hope, on the note of salvation.

Verses 9-20 describe that salvation in the Millennial Kingdom, the Kingdom which Jesus will bring when he comes again. While the focus of these verses is on what will be true when the King of Israel is in her midst, when Christ returns to the earth, we are also reminded of what is true in salvation right now.

The true character of future salvation is already on display in the present, not to the same degree, not in a finished way, but the nature of it is already a reality. Though we await glorification, the great transformation of spiritually dead people into true worshippers has already occurred, and the result is that saved people are CHANGED people. Saved people are citizens of a Heavenly Kingdom and true subjects of the Divine King.

As we look at what God says about the future, we can also cast a thankful and an examining eye on the present. We can give thanks to God for His saving work right now. We can ask Him to help us discern where it has really occurred, and we can ask Him to give us many souls in the present who will then share in that great salvation day in the future.

In the end of Zephaniah, we see the promise of salvation (3:9-13) and the song of salvation (3:14-20). In this chapter, we'll look at the promise.

Notice two things about this promise: It is God's work, and it is all spoken of in terms of absolute certainty.

From beginning to end, God says He is the One doing this. Thus, salvation is sovereign and gracious. Since it is of God, salvation is certain. This good and all-powerful God decreed it and has determined to do it. It is based:

- Not on man's initiative, but on God's.
- Not on man's power or ability, but on God's.
- Not on man's merits, but on Christ's.

What is true of the salvation that will be on display at the time that Christ returns, is true at this very moment. If we desire to see people rescued from hell, if we want to see people's lives transformed and to see Christ loved and honored, then we must pray to the one who saves sinners, because He is the explanation for salvation.

Notice the "I wills" of God in the book of Zephaniah,[18] and you will see that the very same God who is acting to judge sin, is the God who is acting to save sinners. In fact, it is interesting that until you get to chapter 3, there are 12 "I will" statements in Zephaniah, and every one of them is a statement by God about what He will do in judgment. In chapter 3, there are 9 "I will" statements, and each is a promise related to salvation.

3:9 *For at that time **I will** change the speech of the peoples to a pure speech...*

---

[18] In Hebrew, the idea of "I will" is expressed as a part of the conjugation of the verb, not as separate words. But it's there.

3:11 *On that day you shall not be put to shame because of the deeds by which you have rebelled against me; for then **I will** remove from your midst your proudly exultant ones...*

3:12 *_I will_ leave in your midst a people humble and lowly...*

3:18 *_I will_ gather those of you who mourn for the festival, so that you will no longer suffer reproach.*

3:19 *Behold, at that time **I will** deal with all your oppressors. And **I will** save the lame and gather the outcast, and **I will** change their shame into praise and renown in all the earth.*

3:20 *At that time **I will** bring you in, at the time when I gather you together; for **I will** make you renowned and praised among all the peoples of the earth...*

In verse 9 of this chapter we see four things that God's saving work will produce in the future: <u>united worshippers</u>, <u>resurrection life</u>, <u>humility</u> and <u>peace</u>. Because the nature of salvation is the same, we can also say there are four things in salvation that God produces when He brings it about in the present. It's not yet perfected, but the nature of it is a reality right now.

GOD'S SAVING WORK WILL PRODUCE UNITED WORSHIPPERS (3:9)

Transformed speech

What is described here is a spiritual transformation, a changed heart, that will result in them calling upon the name of the Lord.

The place where sinfulness is most clearly manifested is the mouth. Our mouths reveal what is in our hearts—our thoughts loves, hatreds, goals, ambitions, allegiances, motives, and everything else about our character. And when the heart is unregenerate and has not been transformed by the power of God through Christ, what comes out of the mouth is the evidence of idolatry. In the following verses and many others, God's Word tells us that the mouth gives expression to wicked hearts.

Isaiah 6:5 And I said: *"Woe is me! For I am lost; for I am a man of unclean lips, and I dwell in the midst of a people of unclean lips; for my eyes have seen the King, the LORD of hosts!"*

Matthew 12:34 *You brood of vipers! How can you speak good, when you are evil? For out of the abundance of the heart the mouth speaks.*

Psalm 10:1 *Why, O LORD, do you stand far away? Why do you hide yourself in times of trouble? ² In arrogance the wicked hotly pursue the poor; let them be caught in the schemes that they have devised. ³ For the wicked boasts of the desires of his soul, and the one greedy for gain curses and renounces the LORD. ⁴ In the pride of his face the wicked does not seek him; all his thoughts are, "There is no God." ⁵ His ways prosper at all times; your judgments are on high, out of his sight; as for all his foes, he puffs at them. ⁶ He says in his heart, "I shall not be moved; throughout all generations I shall not meet adversity." ⁷ His mouth is filled with cursing and deceit and oppression; under his tongue are mischief and iniquity.*

We could give many other Bible references to demonstrate that the mouth gives expression to wicked hearts.

Transformed speech for worship

The picture is of God having purified the speech of the nations. It has been defiled, but now God has changed that. False gods will no longer be on their lips, but Yahweh will be worshipped by them. Notice that the reason for the purified speech is WORSHIP. Please don't miss that. God changes hearts <u>to create worshippers</u>.

John 4:23 *But the hour is coming, and is now here, when the true worshipers will worship the Father in spirit and truth, for the Father is seeking such people to worship him.*

When someone says God has granted them salvation, they are saying that God has changed their heart. If this is true, then it will be reflected in what they say. Their whole worldview has changed, Christ is their Lord and their life is God-centered. This new, purified speech is reflected in worship. Salvation produces a new attitude toward God. We go from being God-haters to God-lovers, from idolaters to worshippers.

United service with other believers

Salvation does not just change hearts toward God; it unites them in the worship and service of God. They will not only CALL upon the name of the Lord (seek the Lord); they will SERVE God together *with one shoulder* (literally)—shoulder to shoulder is the idea. There is something wrong at work in the person who claims salvation but separates himself or herself from the family of God and never finds it possible to function in that family.

Salvation brings us into a community with other people who have been saved and work together. It is very important that we recognize a few things about the community of believers.

The church is a **household** of faith. The qualifications for leadership in the church largely surround the matter of family management. Why? Because the local church is a visible expression of the family of God. The church is the household of God, so it is managed as a family, not as a business.

This household has order and rules and authority. The New Testament is full of evidence that our part in the family of God is not without accountability.[19] In the family of God, there is love and mutual accountability, not only to the elders and deacons, but to each other. You don't live without the expectation that people are going to be involved with your life.

In the New Testament, believers are always found **in this household**. They are not only in churches; they are well-known in their churches. The idea of a Christian bouncing from church to church, like picking a restaurant, is not something you can support in Scripture. Nor will you find believers who decide to just do family worship, or individual worship, without a faithful and accountable relationship to the local church and its leaders.

It is salvation that explains both our desire for one another and our cooperation with one another.

1 John 2:18 *Children, it is the last hour, and as you have heard that antichrist is coming, so now many antichrists have come. Therefore we know that it is the last hour. [19] They went out from us, but they were not of us; for if they had been of us, they would have continued with us. But they went out, that it might become plain that they all are not of us.*

Romans 16:16 *Greet one another with a holy kiss. All the churches of Christ greet you. [17] I appeal to you, brothers, to watch out for those who cause divisions and create obstacles contrary to the doctrine that you have been taught; avoid them. [18] For such persons do not serve our Lord Christ, but their own appetites, and by smooth talk and*

---

[19] See, for example, Acts 6:1-6; 1 Timothy 4:11-12; Hebrews 13:17; James 5:14.

flattery they deceive the hearts of the naive. ¹⁹ For your obedience is known to all, so that I rejoice over you, but I want you to be wise as to what is good and innocent as to what is evil. ²⁰ The God of peace will soon crush Satan under your feet. The grace of our Lord Jesus Christ be with you.

GOD'S SAVING WORK WILL PRODUCE RESURRECTION LIFE (3:10)

God's marvelous power reclaims what was lost and produces the raising up of what was thought dead. One day the nation of Israel will glorify God through salvation in this coming Kingdom. Here we have a picture describing a new day, when a people who were scattered throughout the world as a result of the righteous judgment of God upon their sins, have returned. By the sovereign power and plan of God, they are coming from the far reaches of the earth to worship Him, though it seemed impossible. God's saving plan toward them as a people, as a nation, looked dead, but the gospel of God brought them home.

Ezekiel 37:1 *The hand of the LORD was upon me, and he brought me out in the Spirit of the LORD and set me down in the middle of the valley; it was full of bones. ² And he led me around among them, and behold, there were very many on the surface of the valley, and behold, they were very dry. ³ And he said to me, "Son of man, can these bones live?" And I answered, "O Lord GOD, you know." ⁴ Then he said to me, "Prophesy over these bones, and say to them, O dry bones, hear the word of the LORD. ⁵ Thus says the Lord GOD to these bones: Behold, I will cause breath to enter you, and you shall live. ⁶ And I will lay sinews upon you, and will cause flesh to come upon you, and cover you with skin, and put breath in you, and you shall live, and you shall know that I am the LORD." ⁷ So I prophesied as I was commanded. And as I prophesied, there was a sound, and behold, a rattling, and the bones came together, bone to its bone. ⁸ And I looked, and behold, there were sinews on them, and flesh had come upon them, and skin had covered them. But there was no breath in them. ⁹ Then he said to me, "Prophesy to the breath; prophesy, son of man, and say to the breath, Thus says the Lord GOD: Come from the four winds, O breath, and breathe on these slain, that they may live." ¹⁰ So I prophesied as he commanded me, and the breath came into them, and they lived and stood on their feet, an exceedingly great army. ¹¹ Then he said to me, "Son of man, these bones are the whole house of Israel. Behold, they say, 'Our bones are dried up, and our hope is lost; we are indeed cut off.' ¹² Therefore prophesy, and say to them, Thus says the Lord GOD: Behold, I will open your graves and raise you from your graves, O my people. And I will bring you into the land of Israel. ¹³ And you shall know that I am* the LORD, when I open your graves, and raise you from your graves, O my people. [14] And I will put my Spirit within you, and you shall live, and I will place you in your own land. Then you shall know that I am the LORD; I have spoken, and I will do it, declares the LORD."

What God will do through this great outpouring of salvation, a work that will be witnessed in the Millennial Kingdom, God does right now one soul at a time. He takes lives that are dead in trespasses and sins, makes them alive and brings them home. He breathes life into them, granting not only the forgiveness of their sins, but the very life of His Son. His word comes to them with the power of His breath, and they are raised to life. Has He raised you?

GOD'S SAVING WORK WILL PRODUCE HUMILITY (3:11-12a)

The purifying and purging work of Christ in judgment will leave only one kind of person in the land. It will be a saved person.

The life record of the nation of Israel is one of shame because they have been rebellious. They are the nation of wasted privilege and wasted opportunity. No other people has been graced the way they have. But God, who chose them by His grace, will by His grace and saving power, remove their shameful ways of rebellion and pride.

Isaiah 54:1 *"Sing, O barren one, who did not bear; break forth into singing and cry aloud, you who have not been in labor! For the children of the desolate one will be more than the children of her who is married," says the LORD. [2] "Enlarge the place of your tent, and let the curtains of your habitations be stretched out; do not hold back; lengthen your cords and strengthen your stakes. [3] For you will spread abroad to the right and to the left, and your offspring will possess the nations and will people the desolate cities. [4] "Fear not, for you will not be ashamed; be not confounded, for you will not be disgraced; for you will forget the shame of your youth, and the reproach of your widowhood you will remember no more. [5] For your Maker is your husband, the LORD of hosts is his name; and the Holy One of Israel is your Redeemer, the God of the whole earth he is called. [6] For the LORD has called you like a wife deserted and grieved in spirit, like a wife of youth when she is cast off, says your God. [7] For a brief moment I deserted you, but with great compassion I will gather you. [8] In overflowing anger for a moment I hid my face from you, but with everlasting love I will have compassion on you," says the LORD, your Redeemer. [9] "This is like the days of Noah to me: as I swore that the waters of Noah should no more go over the earth, so I have sworn that I will not be angry with you, and* *will not rebuke you.* [10] *For the mountains may depart and the hills be removed, but my steadfast love shall not depart from you, and my covenant of peace shall not be removed,"* says the LORD, *who has compassion on you.*

God will, through salvation, produce a people who do not relate to Him in that shameful way. He will:

1. Remove the rebellious person
2. Remove the haughty person
3. Leave a humble people
4. Leave a lowly people

This is what God does in salvation right now: change rebellious and proud people into humble and obedient people who have lowly hearts. Salvation never comes to a soul without humility.

GOD'S SAVING WORK WILL PRODUCE PEACE (3:12-13)

The future Kingdom will be one of righteousness and holiness, and as a result, one of peace. It will have:

1. Peace from enemies – God will be their refuge.
2. Peace with men – The treatment of others will be transformed. Injustice, lies, and deceit will be removed.
3. Peace within – Although sometimes people are safe when they don't feel safe, in this day, Israel will know that she is safe.

We can know this kind of peace now. (See Psalm 23 and Luke 12:22-34.) We can know the fear-free, worry-free, anxiety-free life. Why? Because our Heavenly Father cares for us.

7
THE SONG OF SALVATION
(3:14-20)

The book of Zephaniah finishes on a high note. It is so different from the rest of the book that some have wondered whether it was a later addition. This book began with one of the most blunt pronunciations and pictures of God's wrath, but concludes with one of the most awe-inspiring descriptions of love that you'll find anywhere in the Word of God.

It ends with the picture and the promise of salvation and looks ahead to the time of salvation when the King of Israel will dwell in her midst. All her past shame is replaced with worldwide renown, all her fears are comforted, and all the causes of her fears are removed by God.

- It is a <u>gracious thing</u> that God has determined to do. She doesn't deserve it.
- It is a <u>faithful thing</u> that God has determined to do because it is the fulfillment of unconditional covenants sworn by God Himself to the fathers of this people.
- It is <u>an amazing thing</u> that God has determined to do and promises to do. It will involve the reversal of fortunes and the resurrection of a people.

God has already spoken in this book of unsurpassed judgment of this people. (1:1-18), but now He makes plain that the restoration will be equally awe-inspiring. Every blessing described here belongs to the humble remnant that God will create. Verses (11-13):

"On that day you shall not be put to shame because of the deeds by which you have rebelled against me; for then I will remove from your midst your proudly exultant ones, and you shall no longer be haughty in my holy mountain. 12 But I will leave in your midst a people humble and lowly. They shall seek refuge in the name of the Lord, 13 those who are left in Israel; they shall do no injustice and speak no lies, nor shall there be found in their mouth a deceitful tongue. For they shall graze and lie down, and none shall make them afraid."

Then He says: "Sing about this. Shout about this." What we have in verses 14-20 is "The Song of Salvation." There are three things true of God's people in the day when they realize the salvation that God has promised. First, in verse 14 we see the day of salvation. This is the day of the Millennial Kingdom that is promised and will be ushered in by the Messiah Himself. The Lord Jesus returns to the earth, and it's going to be a day of exuberant joy.

THE DAY OF SALVATION IS A DAY OF EXUBERANT JOY (3:14)

Throughout this section we are pointed to a future day, the day of the Lord, in terms of the salvation aspects of that day. This is the day of the Millennial Kingdom that is promised and will be ushered in by the Messiah Himself. The Lord Jesus returns to the earth, and it will be a day of exuberant joy. This exuberant joy is what God commands, and it should characterize redeemed people. Verse 14:

"Sing aloud, O daughter of Zion; shout, O Israel! Rejoice and exult with all your heart, O daughter of Jerusalem!"

There are four imperatives in this verse.

You Sing – Daughter of Zion

Daughter of Zion is a poetical personification, as if the nation were a woman. It calls upon her to sing. When we see personification in the Old Testament, it is usually in a context of intense emotion.

You Shout – Israel

Shout, O Israel!—literally, raise a shout. It's a word that's used in some contexts to refer to the shouting that would be at the beginning of a battle. The One who is saving you is a great warrior, a mighty Savior. He is not coming to do war against you, but He has delivered you, so raise a shout in view of the deliverance that your mighty Warrior Savior has given to you.

Since *Israel* is mentioned, we now see that this daughter is actually a nation of people, and God calls upon them to shout.

You Rejoice – (Israel)

God calls upon them to shout because God calls upon them to rejoice.

You Exult with All Your Heart – Daughter of Jerusalem

The Hebrew term for *heart* was used in three ways. It could refer to the will of a person, to the mind (the intellect) of a person, or to the person's emotions. In this context, it seems to refer to the emotions. God is calling upon the people to give passionate praise for the salvation He has brought them. This is a poetic way of describing the reaction to this amazing salvation in the day when it is revealed. Those who are redeemed will answer this call, and great emotion will be on display from the hearts of a thankful people.

In this day, salvation will be manifested in great joy, not indifference. Indifference indicates our ignorance of salvation. If you can think about it, talk about it, contemplate it, sing about it, preach about it, study about it, and salvation doesn't engage the whole person, you really don't understand it. When people comprehend both what God has graciously done for them and His command to praise Him with great joy, they should be the most joyful, enthusiastic and grateful people on the face of the earth.

Something is wrong when we claim to have salvation, yet we are stoics. We do well to compare our expressions of worship with those we see in Scripture. Emotionalism is not a good thing. Emotionalism is when emotions carry a person away and they are under the control of emotion instead of thoughtfully and truthfully responding to God. But true worship is a genuine response to God for who He is and what He has done. It involves the whole man and certainly engages the heart.

THE DAY OF SALVATION IS A DAY OF GRACIOUS DELIVERANCE (3:15)

The call for rejoicing is followed by the reasons for rejoicing. God's people are characterized not by mindless joy but by a thoughtful joy. It is because God's people are aware of what great things the Lord has done for them that they give passionate praise to God for His goodness to them.

Here prophetic perfect tenses are used that speak of the certainty of these future events. These things are as good as done and are considered as if they are already accomplished.

Judgments Removed

The first reason for great rejoicing is the removal of judgment. This involves forgiveness, but also emphasizes the fact that the time of judgment has passed, and the time of restoration has arrived.

We get a very real taste of what the faithful remnant in Judea knew. If we know Christ, we are a forgiven people. We have been reconciled to God, yet we know what it is to suffer the consequences of sin-sick humanity. We still live in the midst of a world that is under a curse. Whether we talk about sharing with the whole world in the ongoing effects of the fall, or we talk about sharing in the judgments brought upon a disobedient nation, we know that salvation has not spared us from all of sin's repercussions. God's curse is known and felt. But a day is coming when we will have passed through such judgments, and all that will remain is the salvation that God has graciously destined us for. What a day of rejoicing that will be!

Enemies Cleared Away

God has judged the Israelite people at the hands of enemies. When this new day comes and the Messiah ushers in this future glorious kingdom, the day of Israel's enemies having their way with her will be over. God will sweep all of those enemies away. This will be something for the redeemed to sing about and to shout over!

Again, the believers suffered because of the unbelief of the nation. It wasn't just the disobedient and rebellious who would be overrun and taken away by Babylon where they would grieve over the destruction of Jerusalem and the temple. The godly remnant would suffer greatly also. Today, genuine believers often suffer at the hands of the enemies of God and the church, all over the world, but a day is coming when this will end, when there will be no more cause to fear enemies.

The King in Israel's Midst

The history of Israel is the history of God's gracious involvement with that people. The Lord was with her as she was delivered from Egypt and brought into the land of Canaan. He was with her throughout the period of the judges when He delivered her again and again after she had forgotten Him and rebelled against Him. The Lord was with her throughout the times of the kings when He was patient with her, granting her time for repentance. But there would come the time when judgment would fall, and His glory would depart. She would be given over to her enemies. Not only will the future day of salvation be a day of deliverance from enemies, but a day when God will be present in the Messiah Himself. Her Divine King will be in her midst.

Evil No Longer a Cause for Fear

They will no longer have to fear evil, for two reasons. God will have dealt with evil personified in the form of their enemies, and He will have dealt with the CAUSE of this judgment. God will take away their sins, and evil will be purged from her midst. How do we know that? He says, *The LORD is in your midst.* The Lord and evil cannot dwell together.

Psalm 5:4 *For you are not a God who delights in wickedness; evil may not dwell with you.*

Notice how often the language in the Old Testament describes the need to *purge evil* from Israel.

Concerning <u>prophets who urge following other gods</u>:
Deuteronomy 13:5 *But that prophet or that dreamer of dreams shall be put to death, because he has taught rebellion against the LORD your God, who brought you out of the land of Egypt and redeemed you out of the house of slavery, to make you leave the way in which the LORD your God commanded you to walk. <u>So you shall purge the evil from your midst.</u>*

Concerning <u>those who worship other gods</u>:
Deuteronomy 17:7 *The hand of the witnesses shall be first against him to put him to death, and afterward the hand of all the people. <u>So you shall purge the evil from your midst.</u>*

Concerning <u>rebellion against a legal decision by the priests</u>:
Deuteronomy 17:12 *The man who acts presumptuously by not obeying the priest who stands to minister there before the LORD your God, or the judge, that man shall die. <u>So you shall purge the evil from Israel</u>.*

Concerning <u>false witnesses</u>:
Deuteronomy 19:19 *then you shall do to him as he had meant to do to his brother. <u>So you shall purge the evil from your midst</u>.*

Concerning <u>rebellious children</u>:
Deuteronomy 21:21 *Then all the men of the city shall stone him to death with stones. <u>So you shall purge the evil from your midst</u>, and all Israel shall hear, and fear.*

Concerning <u>prostitution or other sexual sin before marriage</u>:
Deuteronomy 22:21 *then they shall bring out the young woman to the door of her father's house, and the men of her city shall stone her to death with stones, because she has done an outrageous thing in Israel by whoring in her father's house. <u>So you shall purge the evil from your midst</u>.*

Concerning <u>adultery</u>:
Deuteronomy 22:22 *"If a man is found lying with the wife of another man, both of them shall die, the man who lay with the woman, and the woman. <u>So you shall purge the evil from Israel</u>.*

Concerning <u>slavery</u>:
Deuteronomy 24:7 *"If a man is found stealing one of his brothers of the people of Israel, and if he treats him as a slave or sells him, then that thief shall die. <u>So you shall purge the evil from your midst</u>.*

The church is a community that should picture the kingdom, in that sin is dealt with in our midst. The Lord is concerned about purity in His church.

1 Corinthians 5:9 *I wrote to you in my letter not to associate with sexually immoral people-- ^{10} not at all meaning the sexually immoral of this world, or the greedy and swindlers, or idolaters, since then you would need to go out of the world. ^{11} But now I am writing to you not to associate with anyone who bears the name of brother if he is guilty of sexual immorality or greed, or is an idolater, reviler, drunkard, or swindler-- not even to eat with such a one. ^{12} For what have I to do with judging outsiders? Is it not those inside the church whom you are to judge? ^{13} God judges those outside. <u>"Purge the evil person from among you."</u>*

THE DAY OF SALVATION IS A DAY OF GLORIOUS COMFORT (3:16-20)

A Comforted People (3:16)

Evil is gone. There is no reason to fear or have weak hands. They are to be encouraged and be comforted. Kenneth Barker comments:

> The expression "do not let your hands hang limp" is unfamiliar to our culture. In Hebrew thought the hand symbolized strength or power. Letting the hands hang limp referred to a feeling of weakness or powerlessness, a sense of discouragement. In other contexts, hands hanging limp or being "gone" (Deut 32:36) indicated loss of power. Thus "the Lord's salvation is comprehensive: fear is banished as to its objective causes (3:15: 'evil'), its subjective reality (3:16: 'not fear'), and its immobilizing effect (listlessness).[20]

A Celebrated People (3:17) (Deut. 30:9)

This description of God is very much like the delight and rejoicing of someone who takes a bride.

Isaiah 62:1 *For Zion's sake I will not keep silent, and for Jerusalem's sake I will not be quiet, until her righteousness goes forth as brightness, and her salvation as a burning torch.* ² *The nations shall see your righteousness, and all the kings your glory, and you shall be called by a new name that the mouth of the LORD will give.* ³ *You shall be a crown of beauty in the hand of the LORD, and a royal diadem in the hand of your God.* ⁴ *You shall no more be termed Forsaken, and your land shall no more be termed Desolate, but you shall be called My Delight Is in Her, and your land Married; for the LORD delights in you, and your land shall be married.* ⁵ *For as a young man marries a young woman, so shall your sons marry you, and as the bridegroom rejoices over the bride, so shall your God rejoice over you.*

God's delight in them will be the fulfillment of His decrees concerning

---

[20] Kenneth L. Barker, *Micah, Nahum, Habakkuk, Zephaniah*, vol. 20, The New American Commentary (Nashville: Broadman & Holman Publishers, 1999), 495.

them. It reflects the delight that God promised after deliverance from exile.

Deuteronomy 30:1 *"And when all these things come upon you, the blessing and the curse, which I have set before you, and you call them to mind among all the nations where the LORD your God has driven you, ² and return to the LORD your God, you and your children, and obey his voice in all that I command you today, with all your heart and with all your soul, ³ then the LORD your God will restore your fortunes and have mercy on you, and he will gather you again from all the peoples where the LORD your God has scattered you. ⁴ If your outcasts are in the uttermost parts of heaven, from there the LORD your God will gather you, and from there he will take you. ⁵ And the LORD your God will bring you into the land that your fathers possessed, that you may possess it. And he will make you more prosperous and numerous than your fathers. ⁶ And the LORD your God will circumcise your heart and the heart of your offspring, so that you will love the LORD your God with all your heart and with all your soul, that you may live. ⁷ And the LORD your God will put all these curses on your foes and enemies who persecuted you. ⁸ And you shall again obey the voice of the LORD and keep all his commandments that I command you today. ⁹ The LORD your God will make you abundantly prosperous in all the work of your hand, in the fruit of your womb and in the fruit of your cattle and in the fruit of your ground. For the LORD will again take delight in prospering you, as he took delight in your fathers ..."*

Not only does the Lord delight in His people—He quietly loves them. The middle statement there, "He will quiet you by His love" is extremely difficult in the Hebrew text. People have rendered and explained this in at least six different ways. It is best to just take it in its most straightforward sense. The word *you* is not literally in the text, and this particular verb is most often used in a sense that it refers to something happening in the one who is exercising it. He's not causing quietness, but there's quietness in Him. So, the idea is this: Since God delights in His people, He rejoices over them with gladness, quietly contemplating that delight in them! Finally, there is a joyous outburst of song over them from God. We see then, the people of God are to sing the songs of joy (:14) to the God who takes joy in them (:17)! Are you amazed that God loves you, takes delight in you and rejoices over you?

A Restored People (3:18-20)

Now God speaks to them personally. It is one thing to hear comforting words about God's dealings with you, but it is another thing to hear comforting words from the God who is dealing with you. Among these verses are six redemptive "I wills", things that God is going to do.

1. *I will gather* into the place they long for (3:18) (remove sorrow)

He pictures those people having been dispersed, mourning for those group gatherings that they once knew in their land. They're mourning for the days of festival and for worship at the temple.

2. *I will deal* with all those who oppress them (3:19) (relieve oppression)
3. *I will save* the lame *and gather* the outcast (3:19) (regather the dispersed)
   J. A. Motyer said it well: "No personal inability will be allowed to prevent the Lord's pilgrims from coming safely home. Rather, the Lord will provide everything necessary for them (Isa 42:16; Jer 31:7–9)."[21]
4. *I will change* their shame into renown (3:19) (cf 3:11) (receive honor)
   This won't be merely superficial. God will change their reputation by changing them from being a shameful people, to an obedient people. In Deuteronomy 30, God said He will circumcise them in heart. He will cause them to love Him, and they will be a gem of His grace, a manifestation of His saving power.
5. *I will bring* you into your land – home (3:20) (restore fortunes)
6. *I will make* you renowned among all peoples (3:20)
7. *When I gather* (3:20) (God is the one who does all of this.)
8. *When I restore* (3:20) (He will make them prosper again.)

All of this has lessons for Israel and for us, the church. For Israel:

- God's saving work is greater than her sins – He will put away her judgment.
- God's saving work is greater than her emotions – fears without and fears within.
- God's saving work is greater than her enemies – God will clear them all away.
- God's saving work is greater than her reputation – He will produce a changed character in her and make it known.

And for us? God's saving work toward Israel is also a picture of His saving work in us. How has our God shown Himself greater than in our salvation? It is greater than our sins, our feelings, our enemies, and our past and our reputation. This is all explained by God's sovereign will and His love. He is the Lord, and He has spoken!

---

[21] As quoted in Barker, p. 499.

8
STUDY GUIDE

Lesson 1 – More Than Reformation – 1:1 (Overview)

Reading to Prepare:
Read all three chapters of Zephaniah in one sitting.
2 Chronicles 33 and 34

1. Who was king of Judah when Zephaniah gave this prophecy? What century was this?
2. What was the general nature of King Manasseh? Of King Amon? Of King Josiah?
3. What do we know about the man Zephaniah? Who may have been his relative?
4. What does the book of Zephaniah teach us about reforms?
5. What three parts are there in the book of Zephaniah?
6. Why is reform not enough?
7. Have you merely reformed your life, or have you truly repented? That is, are you merely trying not to be too awful, or has God given you a new nature, so that you are longing to follow Him?
8. Do you aim for and look for signs of genuine repentance in your own life?
9. Do you aim for and look for signs of genuine repentance in the lives of others?
10. What signs of genuine repentance can we learn from 2 Corinthians 7:8-11?
11. What do you need to say to the Lord concerning your repentance?
    - Do you need to thank Him for it?
    - Do you need to confess to Him that you've never really repented?
    - Do you need to ask Him to make it deeper?

Lesson 2 – Judgment Now and Judgment to Come – 1:2-13

Reading to Prepare:
    Zephaniah 1
    Luke 13:1-5
    Obadiah 1:15
    Genesis 6:7
    Jeremiah 25:31-33
    2 Samuel 5:1-5

1. How do disasters and even accidents point toward God's judgment in the future?
2. When someone has a tragedy, does that mean that the person was particularly sinful?
3. What event or time is mentioned at least 19 times in the book of Zephaniah?
4. What does "the Day of the Lord" mean to you? What thoughts or emotions does it bring to mind?
5. What is an appropriate response to the prophets' warnings concerning the Day of the Lord?
6. In what way can the Day of the Lord announced by Zephaniah be considered a reversal of the creation of the world?
7. How is Judah's destruction related to the worldwide destruction of the last days?
8. Think of two or three or four of your greatest achievements or goals—perhaps things you've made or hope to make, things acquired or accomplished, or honors received. Which of these will survive in the Day of the Lord?
9. In what five realms had Judah violated the Lord's covenant, so that He will judge in those areas?
10. Judah tried to mix worship of the true God with worship of false gods. In what ways today do people try to mix the worship of the true God with false religions?
11. Note the difference between
    (a) modifying a custom of a false religion and giving it a Christian meaning, and
    (b) adopting a custom of a false religion completely, without giving it a Christian meaning.
    Will true Christians disagree at times about customs that fall in group (a)? If so, why?
12. What was wrong with their government leaders?

13. Who are your role models concerning your appearance? What might your desires regarding appearance reveal about the inclinations of your heart?
14. Styles change. What principles would apply equally to such things in 630 BC, in 1600 AD, and today?
15. Can you think of any current example of oppression? (Are you oppressing anyone?) How does knowledge of God's pending judgment change how we view oppression?
16. What will happen to the businessmen? Do you believe putting an end to the city's business should be viewed as a blessing or as a curse?
17. What was the foolish theory of those who were complacent?

Lesson 3 – Only God Can Save From God – 1:14-2:3

<u>Reading to Prepare</u>:
    Zephaniah 1:14-2:3.
    Psalm 90:11
    Revelation 6:12-17
    Deuteronomy 4:9-27

1. What makes a person or a thing a <u>type</u>? What do we mean when we say something in the Bible is a type?
2. This chapter says that "Only God can save from God." What does that mean? Have you ever thought about being saved from God?
3. In what sense was the day of the Lord near and approaching fast?
4. In what way is the day of the Lord near and approaching fast for us? (See 2 Peter 3:1-13.)
5. Review the descriptions in 1:14-16. Are you likely to see them on a calendar or a poster or in verse-of-the-day quotes? Why or why not? Why does it matter?
6. Would Judah be able to escape?
7. How can we survive the day of the Lord's judgment?
8. What five characteristics of true repentance are listed?
9. Do you see these in your life? Do you urge others to have these marks?
10. How does Jesus make it possible for us to survive God's judgment? (Read John 3.)

Lesson 4 – Judgment on the Nations – 2:4-15

Reading to Prepare:
    Read Zephaniah 2.
    Genesis 12:1-3
    Genesis 22:15-18
    Ezekiel 21:1-16

1. The judgments will fall on the nations on all sides of Judah: west, east, south and north. What should they learn from that?
2. The Cherethites were a sub-group of what group?
3. What will be the result of their judgment?
4. Imagine that this was to happen in the next county or state to yours. What would you think or feel?
5. The Moabites and the Ammonites descended from whom?
6. What were their sins?
7. Is it good to be proud of your family, your church, your school, your community, and your nation? Why or why not?
8. Where did the Cushites live?
9. What was to be their judgment?
10. Describe Nineveh, the capital of Assyria. Did anything about the description surprise you?
11. Why was Zephaniah's prophecy concerning Nineveh shocking?
12. What are some of the differences between earthly kingdoms and the Lord's kingdom?
13. What practical bearing does all of this have on our lives?

Lesson 5 – On the Brink of Ruin – 3:1-8

Reading to Prepare:
    Read Zephaniah 3
    2 Kings 23:24-27

1. The Bible says in Romans 8:1, "There is therefore now no condemnation for those who are in Christ Jesus." We know that's true. We also know that God hates sin wherever He finds it and that He judges sin without respect of persons—as with Jerusalem in this chapter and as with churches in Revelation 1-3. How do these two truths fit together?
2. Why is it sometimes easy to hate sin in others, but to excuse it in ourselves?
3. What three charges does the Lord bring against Jerusalem in 3:1?

4. 3:2 lists signs of the city's rebellion. What sign of rebellion is mentioned first? Have you ever seen that sign in yourself?
5. What character qualities or flaws impact a person's willingness to accept correction? What are some ways you could tell whether you're willing to accept needed correction?
6. This commentary says, "To believe God means I don't believe me." Have you ever thought about this idea before?
7. In what areas are you tempted not to believe God?
8. What would be some of the signs of a church full of people who were not really drawing near to God?
9. How do these other sins lead to oppression?
10. 3:4 says, "Her priests profane what is holy." What does that mean?
11. Do you think your religious involvement and your religious activity is pleasing to God while you refuse to believe Him and to honor Him by the way you treat others? (If you do, then you walk in the footsteps of those whom Zephaniah condemned.)
12. How does the Lord's faithfulness make the people's sin even more shameful?
13. Will you listen to Him? Believe Him? Yield to Him? Draw near to Him? Repent of any mistreatment of others?

Lesson 6 – The Promise of Salvation – 3:9-13

Reading to Prepare:
Read Zephaniah 3:9-20.
Isaiah 11 and 12
Revelation 20
Matthew 12:34

1. When you think of Jesus' return, do you usually think of His judgment or His salvation? Or do you usually think of both? Or do you rarely think of His return?
2. What do you know about the Millennial Kingdom from the passages in Isaiah and Revelation?
3. Who brings about the salvation spoken of in Zephaniah 3?
4. Why is that important?
5. What kind of changes happen in a person who is saved? What changes have you seen in your own life as a result of salvation?
6. In what way does a person's speech reveal his or her spiritual condition?
7. "God changes hearts to create worshippers." Is that idea new to you? How can that idea impact the way we do evangelism?

8. What is the difference between united service with other believers and just doing good deeds?
9. Since the church is God's household, what can we conclude about people who claim to love God but hate the church? If you've been severely wounded by a particular church, what is a Biblical way to view God's church as a whole?
10. What seemingly impossible thing is described in 3:10? (And where was Cush?)
11. Does the Bible urge us to be proud or to be humble? (See James 4:6 and 1 Peter 5:5.)
12. When facing a challenge, if we aren't to be proud, where does our confidence come from? (See Psalm 46:1-3.) And how does pride relate to being put to shame?
13. Zephaniah 3:12-13 speaks of a people who are humble and lowly, yet who are unafraid, like sheep that graze and then lie down. How is it possible for people to be full of humility yet full of peace?

Lesson 7 – The Song of Salvation – 3:14-20

Reading to Prepare:
Read Zephaniah 3:9-20.
Psalm 126:3
Revelation 18:20
Psalm 85:3

1. Near the beginning of this chapter are three bullet points. How can those same three words be applied to what God has determined to do for you?
2. Would anyone ever describe your worship as exuberant? If not, what may that say about your relationship to the Lord? Could the commands to Jerusalem in 3:14 help you worship?
3. Have God's judgments been removed from you? If so, what does it mean to you?
4. In what sense can we say that our enemies have already been cleared away and our King is with us? In what sense has that not yet happened?
5. How does the promise of the Lord in her midst relate to her future purity? What does that say to us and to our churches?
6. Do you ever think of the Lord someday having quiet love for his people and also exulting over them with singing? What will that mean?
7. Imagine that you live in ancient Jerusalem in Zephaniah's day and that you've just heard him proclaim all of the judgments that are to

fall on your city because of its sins. Now read through Zephaniah 3:14-20 aloud with that in mind. What are your thoughts or reactions?

8. Zephaniah 3:19 speaks of the Lord changing their shame into praise and renown in all the earth. Has shame been a problem for you? And what is the danger of merely trying to ignore your shame, blasting through it? (See 1 Timothy 4:2)

9. Now imagine yourself as a persecuted Christian or as a Christian living in a very polluted society where almost everyone has gone astray. Read through Zephaniah 3:14-20 aloud again, with the future kingdom of the Lord Jesus in mind. What are your thoughts or reactions?

ABOUT THE AUTHOR

Richard Caldwell Jr. is the senior pastor at Founders Baptist Church in Spring, Texas. He has served in pastoral ministry since 1984. He and his wife Jacquelyn have been married for 34 years and give joyful thanks for their children and grandchildren. Richard is a graduate of Southwestern Baptist Theological Seminary (M.Div.) and The Master's Seminary (D.Min.). He serves as the campus pastor for the Expositor's Seminary's Houston campus. Walking in Grace Media Ministries is the preaching and print ministry of pastor Caldwell.

www.ingramcontent.com/pod-product-compliance
Lightning Source LLC
Chambersburg PA
CBHW071630040426
42452CB00009B/1567